D1246085

warr;or21

A 21-Day Practice for Resilience and Mental Health

Increase your:

Resilience

Inner Strength

Mental Health

You got this!

Jeff Thompson, Ph.D.

ISBN: 978-1-7165-0851-6 (sc)
ISBN: 978-1-7165-0850-9 (e)

Library of Congress Control Number: 2020922687

Because of the dynamic nature of the Internet, any web addresses or links contained in this book may have changed since publication and may no longer be valid. The views expressed in this work are solely those of the author and do not necessarily reflect the views of the publisher, and the publisher hereby disclaims any responsibility for them.

General breathing practices and programs like **warr;or21** are not a replacement for any form of therapy, nor are they intended to cure, treat, or diagnose medical conditions.

The contents of the **warr;or21** program, such as text, graphics, images, breathing practices, and other material contained in the program ("content"), are for informational purposes only. The content is not intended to be a substitute for professional advice or treatment. Always seek the advice of your mental health professional or other qualified health provider with any questions you may have regarding your condition. Never disregard professional advice or delay in seeking it because of something you have read in this program.

If you are in crisis or you think you may have an emergency, call your doctor or 911 immediately. If you're having suicidal thoughts, call 1-800-273-TALK (8255) to talk to a skilled, trained counselor at a crisis center in your area at any time (National Suicide Prevention Lifeline). You can also text TALK to Crisis Text Line at 741741. If you are located outside the United States, call your local emergency line immediately.

Lulu Publishing Services rev. date: 11/18/2020

Contents

Introduction

Congratulations for taking this twenty-one-day journey. The **warr;or21** journey has been designed to help you with managing your thinking, calming
your mind, and building resilience and mental strength. The **warr;or21**
program was inspired by the findings from numerous resilience research studies.[1] Initially created for law enforcement officers and other first responders,
warr;or21 has now been adapted for people from all walks of life across the
globe. We all experience daily stressors, crisis events, and struggles at work.
This program includes practices to help you handle those moments, while also
helping you develop habits to promote an overall better and happier lifestyle.

Regardless of your employment, it is certain that each day includes the opportunity to help others and also look out for your own well-being. Think
about this, and reflect on it. You have an innate desire to help others.
That is partially why are you are participating in **warr;or21**. Remember
though, much like how during an emergency on an airplane, you have to
put on your oxygen mask before helping others, this is no different. To
be effective at helping others, it must start with you. That is not selfish;
in fact, it is necessary. It is also strategic.

Additionally, you have made the choice to take this twenty-one-day path.
Whatever the reason may be—curiosity, wanting to try something new,

---

[1] To learn more about the numerous research studies that contributed to the development of the **warr;or21** program and that support the design and practices, go to
www.warrior21.com/research.

wanting to be more effective at what you already do, or something else (hey, even if someone nudged you to take it!)—you decided first and foremost to purposely take care of yourself. Again, there is nothing selfish about wanting that. To do good in this world, be successful, protect others, and take care of those close to you, you have to first take good care of yourself.

Of course, work and life will get in the way at times, but that does not mean it is okay or healthy to disregard your well-being in the name of helping others. For example, not getting enough sleep, having bad eating habits, not engaging in physical activity, and isolating yourself from others are just a few examples that over time will diminish your ability to do your work effectively and function properly. This also can have a negative impact on your personal life. So, the win-win cliché is in effect here.

Taking care of yourself makes you more effective at your work. It is okay to have bumps in the road. Experiencing hardships, setbacks, and failures is part of living. This journey will give you practices to ensure that those moments do not turn into roadblocks or leave you feeling permanently stuck. We all feel stuck at times; that is normal. **Warr;or21** is about planning to avoid that, and when we do get stuck, having established practices and creating positive coping habits to bounce back, not quit—to persevere.

Resilience is being able to bounce back in a positive manner from adverse situations and life events, often ones that we did not anticipate. Resilience requires taking care of ourselves to ensure we are prepared to handle the stress and unpredictability of our daily lives. Resilience also requires having practices and strategies to handle tough moments in our personal lives.

Importantly, having resilience *does not* mean we can't reach out for help when things feel overwhelming, we feel out of control, or we cannot cope. It is not necessary to take on challenges by yourself when things feel overwhelming or are spinning out of control. It is okay to ask for help. Don't forget: that too is what resilience means.

As part of **warr;or21**, resilience is covered through four pillars that are incorporated in each day: awareness, wellness, purpose, and positivity. Awareness starts with our breathing, yet it also takes into account our thoughts, emotions, and actions. Wellness refers to looking after our physical and mental health, taking care of ourselves. Purpose reminds us that it is okay to have personal goals, yet our work involves much more than just ourselves. We are part of something much bigger, and what we do can affect many people. Finally, positivity refers to the relationships we have with others professionally and socially. It is also about our perspective on our daily interactions and remembering to express gratitude. A key to being positive is realistic optimism. This type of optimism is about working our hardest to achieve practical goals. Through hard work, we realize those goals can be achieved, yet they are not guaranteed simply because we work hard. We can improve our mental health through practice.

Through these four pillars, the **warr;or21** practice not only will provide you with an opportunity to become more effective at your work, but more importantly, it will provide you the opportunity to be more positive, calmer, and happier in your everyday life as you better manage your emotions. You deserve this. There is nothing soft about those terms either. After all, **warr;or21** is designed to enhance your inner strength. We are not machines, and regardless of your work, it is sure to include stress moments. We are bound to experience traumatic situations in all of our lives.

Suppressing and ignoring our experiences and emotions might feel beneficial in the short term, but research has consistently demonstrated that it has a negative impact on our physical and mental health, our social life, and our work. Being sharp and ready for our work is necessary to keep ourselves and others safe. Yet we cannot be on edge twenty-four seven; that is not healthy. Nor is it possible to constantly be like that. Constant hypervigilance takes a toll on our emotional, cognitive, and physiological health.

Further, quality of life is important and something you deserve regardless of your age or employment. Quality of life and being prepared for work are closely interconnected.

Understanding Key Terms: Emotions, Control, Perspective, Empathy, and Pausing

There are important terms that we must understand and be able to practice, using each of them to increase our resilience and mental health. Some key terms are *emotions, control, perspective, empathy*, and *pausing*. Each is incorporated throughout the twenty-one days. Briefly, they are described below.

You do not need to be an expert in psychology, but it is important to have a basic understanding of key psychological terms. Our *emotions* and *feelings* are the result of our thoughts. Our emotions are one of the factors that guide and dictate our actions. We have to acknowledge our emotions—not suppress them—to have better control over them and our actions. So, critical to these twenty-one days is acknowledgment of our emotions so that we can manage them. This is about more than being happy; it is about accomplishing our goals, becoming more resilient, and being successful.

We have to realize and accept what we can *control* and what we cannot. Having practices to control ourselves (our thinking, emotions, and actions) can lead to better coping strategies for crises, stressful moments, and daily interactions. These strategies are especially important for coming to terms with and accepting what we cannot control. We cannot control everything happening around us, but we can control and manage our thinking, emotions, and actions.

Perspective reminds us that even though multiple people may be involved in the same situation, their experience of it is going to be different, as it is shaped by each person's perspective. A perspective can be shaped by someone's life experiences as well as their current emotions and feelings. Perspective allows us to stop and realize this. It often includes suspending judgment, at least temporarily, and avoiding looking at someone else's perspective as right or wrong.

Why see someone else's perspective and suspend judgment? It is strategic. It allows us to further understand what they are thinking and feeling and why they are acting the way they are. This is the essence of *empathy*. Having empathy is critical to being successful in anything we do.

For example, if our goal is to influence others, we are better able to affect their actions if we understand why they are doing what they are doing. By the way, this process is the foundation of hostage negotiation training and has been given to law enforcement hostage negotiators across the world. (I should know; I'm a former negotiator and trainer.) It is not through manipulation either. This type of influence leaves the other person feeling good about the process and not tricked or cheated.

Having empathy does not mean putting aside our own thoughts, feelings, or actions. Understanding the other person's perspective allows us to respond (note, not *react*) accordingly in a way that is best for us.

Finally, *pausing* is connected to everything already mentioned as well as the name of this program: **warr;or21**. The warrior concept should connote perseverance, grit, determination, and resilience. Being a warrior means not giving up. It does not mean mindlessly and recklessly going about things that hurt ourselves and others, causing chaos through our thoughts and actions.

Instead, the **warr;or** concept is about being thoughtful and developing your inner strength. The **warr;or** concept means you have prepared, there is a plan, and you have the ability to adapt. Being adaptable is important because not everything can be predicted, and things do not always go according to the plan. That is where the **;** comes into play. The semicolon is a pause. It is not a comma (or continuation) or period (the end). Rather, while we are in a moment of life, we stop and pause. We control ourselves in the moment to ensure our thoughts are accurate, our emotions are accounted for, and our actions are purposeful. That is the essence of **warr;or21**.

We practice pausing at moments throughout each day to make certain we are looking out for ourselves and our well-being. When we do this, the positive benefits don't stop with us; they continue to spread to others as well.

So, what exactly does this program entail? The **warr;or21** program is twenty-one days of various practices. The daily practices are guided by a different keyword each day and include a morning breathing exercise, a short writing on the keyword, a purposefully selected quote for the day, a reflection practice based on the keyword, and an evening gratitude practice. In total, each day's activities are designed to take only ten to fifteen minutes.

Regardless of how busy you are, even if you have a lot going on that particular day, there will be time to do each of them—if you make the time for it.

The keywords for each day are as follows:

1. Breathe	12. Stress
2. Cognitive Triangle	13. Empathy
3. Calm	14. Sympathy
4. Grit	15. Awe
5. Gratitude	16. Perspective
6. Pause (;)	17. Smile
7. Practice	18. Adapt
8. Resilience	19. Mindfulness
9. Wisdom	20. Silence
10. Emotions	21. Journey
11. Reflection	

The twenty-one days make up a journey where each practice is connected to the previous as well as the next. You are building short goals and achievements, and each contributes to a larger goal (more on this later). The objective is not to be focused on the final twenty-first day. Instead, the goal is to be present in each moment of each day, and that will contribute to an overall goal.

Daily goals work toward a larger goal. The purpose of each day is to enjoy the practices. Remember, it is about perspective. Even if something feels a bit awkward, strange, or even silly, give it a chance. Practice it with an open mind. Be willing to accept that each practice can provide you with something that will help you. Also realize that your appreciation of these practices might not happen instantly. It is a process and journey, so the insight and appreciation might occur later on. As opposed to feeling like it is a chore (for the record, that is not the feeling I am trying to invoke), this open-mindedness will help you move along the twenty-one-day path smoothly and effectively.

This is about resilience. Resilience requires developing a practice to handle tough moments and an overall daily practice that builds our mental health.

How to Use This Book

There are a variety of ways to use this book and its practices. However, the recommended format is to read one chapter per day, as each chapter is dedicated to a particular day and keyword.

Remember, don't be too hard on yourself either. If you miss a day or two throughout the process, that is normal. Being hard on yourself will have a negative impact on you in many ways. Neuroscience research shows this to be the case, and we get into this during the **warr;or21** journey.

If you miss a chapter, catch up when you can. Don't forget: it is your journey, so support yourself while you are doing it. That said, here's a bit of advice: don't let too many days go by without practicing, as it will make it that much harder to pick it back up.

Some have chosen to do twenty-one straight days, while others have spaced it out over longer weeks—for example, doing it Monday through Friday and taking the weekend off as a break. No matter your choice, have a plan and stick with it. Push yourself while you also make sure to enjoy it.

If you would like to take this journey with others, you can sign up to be part of an online group at www.warrior21.com. Past participants have come from all over the world, including the US, Australia, Brazil, Canada, New Zealand, Spain, and the United Kingdom.

Past participants in the **warr;or21** journey said it helped increase their personal resilience, motivation, gratitude, and control over their emotions and actions. People reported feeling calmer and an overall increase in their mental health while also feeling less stressed. [1]

This **warr;or21** program can change you for the better. One person described it the following way: "It gave me a fresh start … it's a line in the sand for me—myself before the course and after the course." [2]

No matter who you are or what you are going through, this book and its practices can help with the daily stressors of life and more significant and impactful events. Here is some feedback from people who took the **warr;or21** journey during the COVID-19 global pandemic and the positive impact the program had:

"Thank you for inviting me to complete this program. It has provided me with a sense of calm and normalcy in this unprecedented time."

"This program has come at the most important time and has a deeper meaning than any of us could have ever expected."

"I have been stressed and on edge worrying about my family and their health during this pandemic. This program has made me take time out of my day for myself."[3]

Finally, the following comment shows resilience yet again, and **warr;or21** is about looking after yourself and others:

"I sincerely believe that this program helped me to deal with stressors in a more thoughtful and meaningful way, and strengthening my resilience allowed me to be there for others."[4]

You decided on this journey. Be ready to embark on a process where you can gain greater control over your thinking, increase your ability to calm your mind, and see a growth in your mental health.

Congratulations! You made it this far.

Your reward is moving onto the next step.

Day 0 helps prepare you for the first practices prior to starting day 1.

Day 0

Stop waiting for the perfect day. Make today the right day to start.

BEFORE YOU CAN BEGIN, YOU have to have a negotiation with
yourself. Really, you need to make a deal, and it is with yourself and
no one else. This takes a level of trust, and if you are this far into **war-
r;or21**, it means we have a developed some level of trust already and
you are willing to try some things, most likely things you have never
tried before.

Thank you.

Thank you for already pushing yourself and venturing outside your comfort zone. That is where real growth occurs. As you will read on day 16, it
is all about perspective. One person can view this as daunting and scary,
yet the person with grit (day 4, by the way) sees that anxiety more as an
opportunity and a challenge that they are ready to take on.

Remember, all I am asking you to do, especially if something feels odd,
uncomfortable, or even silly, is to try it. Trust that I have a reason for
asking you to try it. With that mind-set, let us move on to the first
practice.

Notebook

You will need a notebook as part of your twenty-one-day journey. The notebook is needed for your reflections and your daily, evening gratitude practices. Keep the notebook with you throughout the day to keep track of your thoughts and any ideas that come to mind.

You can use any small notebook that you choose. Alternatively, you can use the pages in the back of this book as your notebook. In the back of this book are pages numbered for you to write down your daily practices as well as the breathing practices this book will discuss.

When you write down your gratitude practice for each day, always start on a new page on the right-hand side of the notebook.

Practice 1: It's Time to Make a Deal

Start with the first page of your notebook, or if you are using this book, the page in the back titled "Day 0." You are going to make a deal with yourself by writing down one of the following two options on the paper. Write down either "I can" or "I can't."

Yes, really.

Write one of them down on the first page of your notebook on the first line. You just made a deal with yourself. When things get busy, which they will, you will make a choice to either stick with this **warr;or21** journey or find an excuse not to do it.

If you write down "I can," you will figure out a way to do it. If you write down nothing and do not do the exercise, or if you write "I can't," you will figure out ways to let things get in the way.

Trust me; you can do this. No matter who you are, I believe in you. You have the strength to do this, as you have already gotten this far. If you tell yourself you can do this, I truly believe you can.

Every day you open your notebook and see the first page, you will be inspiring yourself to push forward. You are becoming your biggest advocate and supporter. You just made a deal with yourself, and no one else knows about it. That said, I have faith in you. You got this!

Practice 2: Have a Goal

I often say in negotiation training that Negotiation 101 tells us to have a goal, while Negotiation 201 reminds us we need a plan to achieve that goal. Well, **warr;or21** is the plan and pathway. Before you begin it though, you have to have a goal. Ask yourself, "What is your overall goal for participating in **warr;or21**?"

This is *your* goal; therefore, there is no right or wrong answer. It is completely up to you. It can be anything you hope to achieve.

Keep in mind this journey is about you and no one else. World peace, as admirable a goal as it is, is not the purpose of this journey. This journey is more about feeling a little bit calmer, a bit happier, or just a bit better about yourself. Write your goal (you can have a few) on the first page of your notebook or on "Day 0" of this book. Write "GOALS" and then list them below. Now every time you open your notebook during these twenty-one days (and beyond), you will be reminded of why you are doing this. If you need to, you can come back during the journey to modify these goals as well.

Now you have officially started your **warr;or21** journey. Congratulations on demonstrating your inner strength and commitment. For day 1 and each day, make sure to try to start your practice in the morning, soon after you wake up. For some, doing all of the practices first thing in the morning won't be possible. Again, all I ask is that you try. At the very least, try to do the breathing practices first thing in the morning. See you tomorrow, and remember—you got this!

Day 1: Breathe

Feelings come and go like clouds in a windy sky.
Conscious breathing is my anchor.
—Thich Nhat Hanh

Note: Today's reading material is a bit longer than the other days because day 1 is important; it's the start of your journey. Day 1 sets your foundation for each successive day. Stick with it; this is the way, and you have arrived. Embrace this with a smile as you move forward. After all, it is all about perspective.

IT ALL STARTS WITH A breath. The essence of **warr;or21** is gaining perspective, building inner resilience, improving your mental health, managing your emotions, and coping with what is beyond your control. The important tool in your toolbox for handling all of that is breathing.

More accurately, controlling your breathing and doing it every day.

Yes, every day.

It sounds simple, yet like most things, it takes practice. And if you are unfamiliar with it, it takes getting out of your comfort zone too. You have to be comfortable with the uncomfortable. Also, having a breathing practice takes time. I get it: you are busy. Make the time. It is only five minutes. It is worth it.

Breathing is the foundation of everything **warr;or21** is about. Regardless of your experience with breathing practices, try the suggestion below.

There is no way around this; there is no shortcut. There also is no magic trick or hidden way to achieve the goals. As silly or as simple as it sounds, it is not just knowing about breathing; it is about doing it and doing it a certain way. This is the foundation of developing new, positive coping strategies and building resilience. You also have to remember that part of developing a new habit, such as this type of breathing exercise, is to enjoy it. There's plenty of neuroscience that I will not go into here, but take my word for it. Just doing the breathing practices is not enough.

Here's how you develop habits such as sticking with your controlled breathing exercises:

1. Tell yourself you're choosing to do it, that you want to do it, and that you are doing it now to work toward a goal (better mental health, for example).
2. Enjoy it while you are doing it. Yes, tell yourself you are enjoying it. It's not designed to be chore!
3. Avoid moving on to your next task right away. Instead, take a few moments (at least twelve seconds) and reflect on why you did it and how it felt doing it. Tell yourself you accomplished it (or use a similar positive phrase, like *succeeded, completed,* or *followed through*) and describe how completing this task will help you care of yourself. Realize that you made the choice to do what you did in order to increase your resiliency and your mental health.

Following these steps will help you develop habits that will stick. Research in neuroscience explains that following these steps will help you effectively develop positive and lasting change. Again, try it, and not just for one day. Habits, after all, need to be repeated.

If you're interested in neuroscience terminology like I am, this is called *experience-dependent neuroplasticity.* You're literally building new neuropathways by following those above steps.

Breathing doesn't fix issues that you are currently facing. This is an important reality check that needs to be pointed out. Instead, breathing practices can help give you clarity to address those issues with a more rational thinking mind, allowing you to figure out what is best for you in the moment and long term.

This is important: breathing does not remove the problems and issues in your life. Rather, it can bring you to a state of mind to best determine how to approach the problems you encounter and decide on a path that is best for you. After all, who knows how best to resolve your issues other than you?

Breathing can serve as an anchor for when the storms of our daily lives become intense and rise beyond our control. It is our constant practice of breathing that will guide us while helping us remain calm and focused; keeping our thoughts, emotions, and actions in check; and deciding how best to proceed.

Morning Practice

Try this breathing exercise for one minute. Breathe in for four seconds through your nostril, then exhale through your nose. Make sure your chest is not expanding when you are breathing in and out. Instead, your breaths should expand and contract your belly area. You can put your hand on your abdomen to feel it, if you'd like.

As you do it, try to think of only the in breath as it happens and then the out breath as you exhale. If your mind wanders, that is fine (it probably will happen, especially if this is new for you). Just recognize that it happened and then go back to your breath. This is your first time practicing it. Remember to enjoy the journey without stressing over the past or worrying about the future—just this moment of breathing in and out.

https://www.warrior21.com/breathe

After completing the breathing exercise, come back and continue reading.

Now that you have finished the one-minute breathing exercise, take a brief moment to reflect on how it felt. Avoid judging the feelings and rather acknowledge how you feel. It is not about right or wrong; instead, it is how you feel. Now focus on the purpose of it: you are taking charge of your mental health, your resilience, and controlling yourself.

Go back to the link and do four more minutes of it. The second version of the animated breathing shield skips the instructions if you do not need them.

After completing the breathing exercise for four more minutes, come back and continue reading.

Now check in with yourself again and reflect on how you are feeling. After doing that (again, it takes only a few seconds), write in your notebook on the back of the first page "Day 1" at the top and write below it five emotions or feelings you have after doing this.

Regardless of what you wrote, tell yourself the following (come on, do it!): "You did it. You accomplished day 1's breathing exercise. This is progress."

More on the Science of Breathing

Why are breathing practices, and more pointedly controlled breathing practices, the foundation of this program and nearly all programs on resilience? There's lots (and lots!) of research demonstrating why breathing practices are so effective.[2]

Breathing practices have been shown to:

- reduce stress
- help you sleep better
- control emotions
- improve attention
- combat feelings of anxiety[5]

After reading the above, do you really need to read more about the benefits of breathing exercises? I'm pretty certain the answer will be no and my persuasion skills have sold you on it, but this stuff (the science of controlled breathing) is fascinating, so I'll share a bit more.

As Christophe André shares in his article,[6] practicing breathing exercises alone is not a silver bullet to resilience, positive mental health, or anything else. There are no silver bullets or one-trick fixes to any of those. Breathing practices are a tool, albeit a very important one, in our toolbox of various techniques and approaches for taking care of ourselves and building resilience.

A word of caution with breathing practices. For some, especially those new to these types of practices, it can create a churn (the turning over or arising of thoughts). What this means is practicing breathing can bring up many things, especially thoughts and memories.

---

[2] Again, if you are interested in the numerous studies behind breathing exercises, check out www.warrior21.com/research.

Dr. Leah Weiss further explains this:

> They think that their self-awareness practice created this churn. Usually though, when they stay with it, they come to realize that the churn was already there; they were just avoiding seeing it.[7]

She adds how breathing practices can be helpful:

> When we begin a mindfulness practice [such as breathing exercises], we are able to see the damaging patterns but we have yet to develop the strength to avoid being overwhelmed by them.[8]

This is what I mentioned earlier. Pushing yourself out of your comfort zone can help you grow a practice to help you not get overwhelmed and have greater mental health, focus, calm, and resilience. The only way past this churn is going through it—and the vehicle to help you navigate it is controlled breathing practices.

Finally, what do you do if your mind wanders or negative thoughts arise while doing your breathing practices (trust me, it will happen)? Dr. Rick Hanson provides practical advice:

> If you get hijacked by the negative material, drop it.[9]

It is normal, regardless of how far along you are in your practice, to have your mind wander or have negative thoughts pop into your mind. That's okay. Just acknowledge it, let it go, and return to concentrating on your breathing. You are on a path and you have the strength to see it through. You are a **warr;or**, and this is the path you have chosen.

Reflection

As you go about your day, come back to the breathing animation if you need to. Try to do it at least once. When you have a free moment, try it out to pause and ground yourself. Remember, it takes practice.

Evening Practice (Near/Close to Bed)

Trust me again with the following practice. Why? Well, first, it is crucial for positive mental health and building resilience. Also, it is going to be your evening practice *every night* for the twenty-one days of this program. It is a gratitude practice (it is the keyword for day 5 and discussed more in depth then), and it helps shape perspective, builds resilience, and increases positive mental health (yeah, basically all the good things!).

It reminds us that there are positive things happening each day in our lives. So, in your notebook, on the next blank right-side page, write "Day 1" at the top and also write down the following:

1. One thing that made you happy *today*
2. One nice thing someone did for you *today*
3. One nice thing you did for someone *today*

Day 2: Cognitive Triangle

No one can make you feel inferior without your consent.
—Eleanor Roosevelt

Morning Breathing Practice

- As early as possible after you wake up, dedicate five minutes of breathing to help you get focused for the day and realize that you are setting your perspective.
- For your first minute of breathing, follow along with this exercise and then repeat for a second minute: https://www.warrior21.com/breathe.
- Set a timer for two minutes and practice four seconds breathing in, four seconds breathing out. Either close your eyes or pick something to fix your eyes on (remember, breathing exercises are about focusing, not drifting off ... or sleeping!).
- Take a brief moment to think about how you are feeling. Don't judge the feeling or emotion; just acknowledge it.
- Click the link again and finish off your practice with one more minute of breathing. Congratulations! That is five minutes of breathing practices accomplished for two days in a row. You're developing a new, healthy habit.
- After you finish, tell yourself, "You accomplished this. You did it."

THE COGNITIVE BEHAVIORAL TRIANGLE, OFTEN used in psychotherapy, can also be used to help us in our daily life. An event (or interaction) leads us to think something, and those thoughts can then lead us to have emotions and feelings, and that results in our actions. Those actions and feelings then impact our thinking, creating a cycle.

The triangle is further explained by Linda Meier Abdelsayed, LMFT:

The Cognitive Triangle is one of the most popular and effective strategies that Cognitive Behavioral Therapists (CBT) use when supporting clients in improving anxiety, depression, and other life-style stressors. The idea behind this strategy is to help you start to connect your thoughts, feelings, and actions ...

By becoming more aware of how all three of these parts of your life affect each other, you can become more aware of how to change things.[10]

The diagram below shows how each is interconnected and influenced by the others. Thus, if we can change one, it can have an impact on the other two.

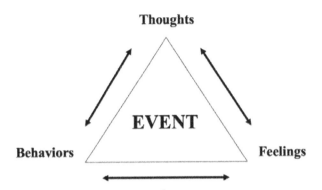

Often, in our daily interactions, we do things quickly or feel like we are on autopilot. This diagram helps us to stop, pause (remember, the ";" is in **warr;or21** for a reason), and reflect on what we are thinking, feeling, and doing. This can help increase our overall awareness. With respect to our thoughts, when we pause, it gives us time to ask ourselves two important questions:

1) Are these thoughts accurate?
2) Are they helpful?

Keep in mind this is not suggesting you second-guess everything that comes into your mind. Additionally, this is not advocating replaying our actions over and over in our heads, thinking about the same event or actions (or actions not taken). This is called ruminating (more on this in day 9) and is not healthy.

The triangle gives you a chance to stop and pause—to ensure your actions are not reactionary but instead are a controlled response. This pause and process of reflecting (along with our breathing practices) builds new wires in the brain. These practices rewire the brain to create new positive habits. This is the heart of what science refers to as the neuroplasticity of the brain. (Dr. Seth Gillihan explains this brilliantly in his book,[11] as does Dr. Alex Korb in his.[12]) The more you practice this, the more your brain becomes accustomed to doing it. This is habit forming, and you are doing it already here on day 2.

Dr. Rick Hanson explains this process:

> Since neurons that fire together wire together, staying with a negative experience past the point that's useful is like running laps in Hell: you dig the track a little deeper in your brain each time you do a lap …
>
> The most direct way to grow inner strengths such as determination, a sense of perspective, positive emotions, and compassion is to have experiences in them in the first place.[13]

Part of reflecting on our thinking is catching us when we fall into what Reivich and Shatté call "thinking traps"[14]—or thinking errors. These cognitive distortions (originally categorized by the great psychologist Dr. Aaron T. Beck) are not helpful and can further push someone down a spiral of distress, anxiety, negative emotion overload, and the sense that things are out of control.

Some of these are described below:

- **Black and white thinking**: Seeing things in an extreme manner, such as always right and always wrong.

- **Shoulding:** This refers to thinking things should be the way we want them to be. An example is "I should have been calmer," "I should have done something differently."
- **Overgeneralization:** Belief that because something happened a certain way, it is always like that.
- **Fortune-telling:** Coming to conclusions based on limited information.
- **Mind reading:** Assuming you know why someone did/didn't do something or why they said something.
- **Entitlement:** Expecting a certain result based on your actions or your status.
- **Discounting the positive:** Focusing only the negative aspects and disregarding any evidence that can contradict that.

How do we avoid these traps and prevent falling into them in the first place? Dr. John Grohol offers the following:

1. **Identify the distortion:** Much like labeling our emotions can be beneficial to managing them, the same process applies here are well.
2. **Shades of gray:** This approach counters some of the traps by avoiding seeing things in absolutes. For example, no one is perfect, including you. You are allowed to make mistakes.
3. **Double standard method:** Make sure you aren't being too harsh on yourself and holding your actions to a much higher standard compared to others. This sounds like a much fairer approach and exactly like something you would say to a friend.[15]

Next, with respect to our feelings, we can pause (day 6) and ask ourselves, "What are the emotions we are (or were) feeling?"

Labeling our emotions and identifying them can help us maintain (or regain) a better understanding of what we are feeling. Even stopping and acknowledging our feelings can help us have a sense of control (or regain control) over ourselves. Seriously, just naming the emotion we are feeling helps make sure it does not dictate our actions or, even worse, control our actions and thinking.

As Dr. Leah Weiss explains, when we stop to reflect on our emotions, it doesn't mean developing a practice that's void of emotions.

Being mindful of your emotions doesn't mean not having emotions. Sadly, this misperception often prevents people from tapping into the wisdom of their emotions ...

If they knew the potential for insight and learning, they wouldn't want to get rid of their emotions even if they could. A major function of mindfulness (day 19) is to help you see emotions for what they are: feedback on the world—no more, no less.[16]

Emotions are further discussed on day 10, but to conclude for now, it is important to emphasize that suppressing or ignoring emotions is not what is being suggested here. It is about acknowledging the emotions and seeking to manage them.

When we pause to reflect on our behaviors and actions, we can determine if we are responding or reacting. Responding connotes something planned and controlled, while reacting is often based on our out-of-control emotions and our lack of thinking or misperceptions. On day 10, we will dig deeper into this. For now though, acknowledging our emotions and labeling them helps prevent them from controlling us. Note, I never said ignore emotions.

Try this: Think of a recent event where you were angry. What were you thinking? How accurate were your thoughts upon reflection, and how was the other person seeing the situation?

With respect to your feelings and emotions, try to name three to five emotions you were experiencing aside from anger. Now think about why you were feeling each of them. This helps you better understand why you were angry (for example, being confused or feeling disrespected). Also note the intensity of those feelings during the interaction and how it most likely has changed by now. This shows that they are fleeting and do not last forever. This practice helps you be better in tune with your emotions, thus helping you manage them better. An added benefit to this practice is that being better in tune with your emotions helps you better understand other people's emotions too. That's empathy, and it is really important.

Finally, consider your behaviors and how you acted. What were your short-term and long-term goals? How were they achieved—or not? Did your actions line up with your morals and integrity? If your behavior and actions contribute to your reputation, especially long after you walk away, how do you want to be known?

These are thought-provoking questions that are intended to increase your awareness of what you do, which can then impact your thinking and restart the entire triangle. We now know that is how it works. The question becomes, How will you use this to your benefit?

The cognitive behavior triangle is one of many tools that allow us to understand how deeply connected our thoughts, emotions, and actions are. It can help you develop new ways of thinking and behaving while accounting for your emotions (again, note that I did not say ignore them). Being mindful and aware of even just one of them – a thought, emotion, or feeling – can have a positive impact on the others. Think about how you can practice this today and going forward. This **warr;or** path is about perspective, and you are expanding yours.

Dig deeper later by exploring at some point today the following two worksheets that explain the cognitive triangle:

Cognitive Triangle—Coping and Processing[17] (Washington.edu)

The Cognitive Model[18] (therapistaid.com)

(Note: Again, real life sets in here. If you don't have time to click the link in the morning, come back to it at some point today.)

Reflection

This is a lot to take in for day 2. If it is all about changing habits, establishing better control over yourself, and enhancing your perspective, you have to get out of your comfort zone. You are doing that. Keep it up. Today, reflect on the cognitive triangle and how it and some of the common cognitive distortions have negatively affected you. Then think about how you can have a better response.

Also, try starting a conversation with someone you know to discuss the triangle. Try to share your perspective with them while also listening to their thoughts on it.

Evening Practice

In your notebook, write down the following on a new, clean page on the right side. Make sure not to repeat your answers to these three questions over the course of the twenty-one days. Try to do this when you are going to bed. It's intended to be (slightly) challenging, as that is what trying something new is—challenging. You got this.

1. One thing that made you happy today
2. One nice thing someone did for you today
3. One nice thing you did for someone today

Day 3: Calm

Your calm mind is your ultimate weapon
against your challenges. So relax.
—Bryant McGill

Morning Breathing Practice

- As early as possible after you wake up, dedicate five minutes of breathing to help you get focused for the day and realize that you are setting your perspective.
- Take the first minute of breathing to follow along with this exercise: https://www.warrior21.com/breathe.
- Set a timer for two minutes and practice four seconds breathing in, four seconds breathing out. As you breathe in, say to yourself, "I am strong." As you breathe out, say to yourself, "I am calm."
- When you are done, take one deep breath.
- Click the link again and do two more minutes of your breathing practice.
- After you finish, think for a moment about your dedication. This is three days in a row. Well done.

YOU ARE STARTING TO GET into a groove now with your new **warr;or21** practice. You might have begun to feel changes and a sense of calm. No worries if not—you're only on day 3!

We all could strive a bit more to increase our ability to remain calm during emotionally driven situations. Remaining calm during those moments helps us focus, see things more clearly, make better judgments, and respond (not *react*) in a manner that is good for us and everyone else. Today, we look beyond our breathing practices (day 1) and our knowledge of the cognitive triangle (day 2).

Being calm connotes professionalism and the ability to not become overwhelmed. Remaining calm takes practice. Again, one effective way to practice being calm is the breathing practices. Today's breathing practice of saying strong/calm also reminds us of how closely the two are connected.

Being calm is something frequently discussed and declared as a necessity, but how is it cultivated? Remember, **warr;or21** is not about soft practices. These approaches are specific for specific results—to increase your resilience and improve your mental health. It is about looking out for yourself and protecting yourself. This can have a positive impact on others and help you to remain sharp.

One example is demonstrating that you are taking care of yourself. One obvious way this is displayed is by remaining calm in tense and emotionally driven situations.

So, how can you prevent adrenaline, stress, and anxiety from controlling you? First, to learn this, we should look to people who work in extremely stressful and tense situations. If you can learn what they do in their unique environments, you can take those skills and adapt them to the situations you find yourself in. One group that all of us can learn from is the US Navy SEALs.

Charles Chu shares "6 Secrets of Mental Toughness from the Navy SEALs":[19]

1. **Eat the elephant:** Take one bite at a time. Don't overwhelm yourself with trying to do everything all at once; instead, break down a massive task into segments.
2. **Visualize success:** This includes positive imagery—picture yourself succeeding (not failing).
3. **Emotional control:** No surprise here, Navy SEALs practice controlled breathing. And again, it is no surprise that one practice is breathing four seconds in and then four seconds out.
4. **Nonreactivity:** Chu reminds us the following of our inner strength:

> We have more control than we think.
>
> We can't control what happens in our outside world, but we can control our interpretation of it.

5. **Think smaller:** Changing perspective is going from seeing everything as negative and impossible to a more positive outlook that sees the little things. Guess what? Yet again, no surprise that Chu describes a practice in gratitude nearly identical to the one you have started doing each day. He says these small victories keep morale high. If you don't believe me yet, put some trust in him:

> Give it [gratitude practices] a shot if you haven't tried this. It matters a lot more than you might think.

6. **Find your tribe (and necessity):** Charles sums this one up neatly with the following (we dig deeper into this too on day 4 with a focus on grit):

We humans are social creatures. And we crave meaning in a world that sometimes seems all too meaningless.

Find both—close friends and close principles—and you have a hotbed for mental resilience.

We aren't Navy SEALs, but we certainly can learn from them, as the above skills are practical enough to be adapted and implemented into our lives. The question is, Will you—and how?

You got this!

Reflection

Today, try to take a moment to reflect on some of the six secrets shared above. Which ones do you feel you do well? Which ones will you work on today? Feel free to write them down, starting on a new page in your notebook, writing "Day 3" at the top.

Evening Practice

In your notebook, write down "Day 3" at the top of a new page on the right side of the notebook and add the following (remember not to repeat any answer you already used on previous days):

1. One thing that made you happy today
2. One nice thing someone did for you today
3. One nice thing you did for someone today

Day 4: Grit

At various points, in big ways and small, we get knocked down.
If we stay down, grit loses. If we get up, grit prevails.
—Angela Duckworth

Morning Breathing Practice

- As early as possible after you wake up, dedicate five minutes to breathing to help you get focused for the day and realize that you are setting your perspective.
- Follow along with this exercise, if needed: https://www.warrior21.com/breathe.
- After you finish, tell yourself (really, say it like this), "You did it."
- Don't forget about building positive habits. The breathing exercise can be challenging, but don't forget to enjoy it.

  o Tell yourself before starting that you are deciding to do this because you want to—it is important to you.
  o Then, while doing it, enjoy the five minutes.
  o Finally, at the end, remind yourself that you just accomplished something, and it was all because you made the time to do it. That should feel good!

- Note: You are doing five minutes of this same breathing exercise today, but know that tomorrow you'll be trying out a new breathing exercise.

WE ALL FAIL IN LIFE. No, I do not mean with everything in life—that is definitely not the purpose of this! Experiencing failure is part of living, as we are not perfect. None of us are. Grit reminds us of our perspective and how we view things. What are we learning? How are we adapting our approaches? How are we persevering and not giving up when we need to continue? Instead of getting stuck and sinking into our faults, our grit answers those questions and gets us back up.

Angela Duckworth, an expert on grit, shares the following:

I do mean hard work and not quitting things when they're hard, but I also mean passion.[20]

Angela Duckworth's work on grit[21] is a must-read for those wanting to delve deeper into the concept of grit and how to apply it to your everyday life. Today we cover key concepts from her book while also getting insight on the topic from Eric Barker. Trust me, you can easily get lost reading many of Barker's articles,[22] and the result will be a deep appreciation for his ability to share research-backed tips in a way that allows you to easily reflect on them and discern how to apply them in your life.

Grit, like resilience, reminds us that we don't have to pick ourselves up on our own. Knowing that you have help and support gives you a perspective that you're not alone and you do not have to solve things by yourself. That is what being part of a gritty group means (more on that below).

Even if you do not enjoy math, the formula below is an easy one. When we experience a hardship with something we are doing, our passion for it helps us to not give up. It's about more than enjoying it. It's called passion for a reason. It is much more meaningful.

The person with grit strives to move forward—not quit—even though it is not easy. Your perseverance is what pushes you forward. This is what

separates people with grit from those without it. We are all certain to experience hardships and challenges. Those with grit will not quit but will instead
push forward. No one said it would be easy, but the person with grit doesn't
look for ways it will fail or immobilize themselves. Instead, they are determined to get through it and make it work. It's the *never give up* mentality.

Passion + Perseverance = Grit

Duckworth shares five components that increase one's grittiness:

1. **Pursue what interests you:** What are your interests—name two
   or three—outside your job?
2. **Practice, practice, practice:** How are you practicing to get better
   at what you do?
3. **Find purpose:** Is your job more than just a job to you? Are you
   doing the necessary things to achieve your short-term goals that
   contribute to your long-term goals being achieved? Are your actions benefiting others?
4. **Have hope:** With hope comes confidence and the ability to continue. This is also connected to realistic optimism (more on that
   with day 16). Do you have faith in your abilities?
5. **Join a gritty group:** This is important. Who's in your gritty
   group? Do you surround yourself, as best as you can, with fellow
   gritty people?

Enjoy what you do for a living. Don't let it just be work. You impact people's lives every day no matter what you do for a living. Questioning how
your work benefits others? Barker helps with that:

I know what some of you are thinking: I want
to be gritty at my job but I don't find meaning in it.

No problemo. Think about what you do that helps others. This alone boosts grit. Beyond that, other research shows that tweaking how you see your job can make a huge difference.[23]

Barker adds in his article the following quote from Duckworth's book:

David Yeager recommends reflecting on how the work you're already doing can make a positive contribution to society ... reflecting on purpose led students to double the amount of time they spent studying for an upcoming exam, work harder on tedious math problems when given the option to watch entertaining videos instead, and, in math and science classes, bring home better report card grades.

Amy Wrzesniewski recommends thinking about how, in small but meaningful ways, you can change your current work to enhance its connection to your core values.[24]

So, doing those five things can increase your grittiness. It will also have another positive impact:

I found that the grittier a person is, the more likely they'll enjoy a healthy emotional life.[25]

Work through the hard aspects, the challenging moments. Use your breathing practices to guide you. Take those moments to pause and reflect throughout the day. You have grittiness in you already. Today's **warr;or21** practices and tips from Duckworth help you articulate what is already inside you.

Reflection

Think of the five aspects of grit mentioned above. Think about how it impacts your way of doing things.

In your notebook, go back to the first page and write down your three strengths connected to how you are already gritty. Look at and reflect on how those strengths will help you achieve the goal you wrote down on day 0.

Evening Practice

In your notebook, write down the following on a new right-side page with today's day (you're doing this every day, so I won't keep repeating this). Remember not to repeat your answers.

1. One thing that made you happy today.
2. One nice thing someone did for you today
3. One nice thing you did for someone today

Day 5: Gratitude

Feeling gratitude and not expressing it is like wrap-
ping a present and not giving it.
—William Arthur Ward

Morning Breathing Practice

- As early as possible after you wake up, dedicate five minutes to breathing to help you get focused for the day and realize that you are setting your perspective.
- Do two minutes of breathing following along with this exercise: https://www.warrior21.com/breathe.
- Now it's time for a new breathing exercise, first created by Dr. Andrew Weil[26] for the 4-7-8 breathing exercise. (Note: access the instructions at www.warrior21.com/478 and remember that the whoosh sound does not have to be loud!)

TODAY'S KEYWORD, *GRATITUDE*, CAN HELP provide a certain perspective as you enter day 5. Yesterday's grit has brought you to today, day 5. The reward is the new breathing practice. I practice it nearly every day … while riding the New York City subway! I didn't start to feel the positive impact until practicing it for just over a week.

To put it simply, it feels good to practice, as it helps remind me that by controlling my breath, I am in control of something. The new breathing practice reminds all of us that it is not about how long you do it for; it is about focus and control. This helps give us a **warr;or** perspective.

If we lose our focus or control, we can simply come back to it (our breathing). Our grit helps us stick with the breathing exercises and the **warr;or21** journey, while gratitude helps us remember to enjoy the process. That is the essence of gratitude—not ignoring the terrible things you might have experienced. It reminds us that there are also good, positive moments throughout the day. That is the purpose of the evening notebook exercise.

Dr. Alex Korb reminds us that gratitude is all about our perspective:

Gratitude is a state of mind—in fact, there's a gratitude circuit in your brain, badly in need of a workout. Strengthening that circuit brings the power to elevate your physical and mental health, boost happiness, improve sleep, and help you feel more connected to other people.[27]

So, what are the gratitude practices that are backed by neuroscience and extensive research?[28] Before we go into it (spoiler alert—it is the evening practice you have been doing for four days already!), let's first examines the benefits of practicing gratitude from Korb:

- decreases depressive symptoms
- reduces anxiety
- improves overall mental health
- improves mood
- increases social support

- improves sleep
- combats negativity
- promotes optimism[29]

Convinced? Ready to start your gratitude practice? Guess what? You have been doing an effective gratitude practice each evening. By writing in your notebook each evening, without repeating your answers, you're wiring your brain to recall positive moments each day. This is how new habits are made and a change in perspective occurs. This also builds resilience and improves your mental health. This truly is the way.

It would be too easy and counterproductive to repeat your answers to the three gratitude questions each evening. Coming up with new answers takes effort (and grit!), and the science shows how beneficial it is too.[30]

From the BBC, on keeping a daily gratitude journal:

Mann stresses that the benefits do not just come from the immediate lift as you write the entries; re-reading your previous entries can help you cope with difficult situations in the future too.[31]

Goodnet.org shares the following research-backed benefits of keeping a gratitude journal (my emphasis added below):

When you take the time to focus on the good things in your life you naturally become more positive.

By writing down what you are thankful for it can make you more optimistic because you are choosing to see more of the positivity in your life and give less power to negative emotions.[32]

The Goodnet.org article further shares that gratitude can prevent you from comparing yourself to others and being resentful of people. Research has also shown that expressing gratitude increases alertness, attentiveness, energy,[33] optimism,[34] and finding meaning and purpose in our work.[35] It also builds resilience, helps us feel socially safer, and can reduce anxiety and fear.[36]

The importance of practicing gratitude is also shown in the research conducted by the great Martin Seligman, founder of positive psychology (as an aside, **warr;or21** would not be complete without mentioning him), as detailed by Dr. Jeremy Dean:

At the end of the day, before you go to bed, spend a few minutes thinking about three good things that happened today. They don't have to be that amazing; just three things that made you feel a little better. You can also think about why they happened.

In one study in which people carried out this exercise, their happiness was increased, and depressive symptoms decreased, fully six months afterwards (Seligman et al., 2005). [37]

We often experience moments and situations that are not positive. Often too, those moments are beyond our control. The gratitude practice does not mean forgetting or ignoring them. It reminds us that there is also good in the world, we are making a difference, and people are doing good deeds for us.

Now you know why you are doing the daily evening practice and how it was inspired by numerous research studies. Enjoy!

Reflection

So now you know why you are writing in your notebook. Think about how it is not a chore; instead, the intention is to create a way of recalling how positive things occur each day. *Make an extra effort to express gratitude to someone today.* Try starting a conversation with someone at some point today to let them know about the gratitude practice. Share with them how it has been going and ask them about their thoughts on it.

Make sure to take time for yourself, to rest and recharge. The minutes are there if you make them available, just as you have been making time for **warr;or21**. Make a deal with yourself—do at least one positive thing for yourself over the next few days. It can be anything, even something small. Just make sure it is for you and that it's something you will enjoy.

Evening Practice

In your notebook, write down the following and remember not to repeat yourself with any of the three questions during the twenty-one days:

1. One thing that made you happy today
2. One nice thing someone did for you today
3. One nice thing you did for someone today
4. After doing this, go back and review your first week's practice in gratitude. Reflect on how it feels to take charge and rewire your brain to enhance your mental health. Write down at least one word to describe how you feel after completing this.

Day 6: Pause (;)

A semicolon is used when an author could've chosen to end their sentence, but chose not to. The
author is you and the sentence is your life.
—Project Semicolon

Morning Breathing Practice

- As early as possible after you wake up, dedicate five minutes to breathing to help you get focused for the day and realize that you are setting your perspective.
- Start off with one minute of the four-by-four breathing (four seconds inhaling and four seconds exhaling). Remember, you can use the animated shield graphic here if you need to: https://www.warrior21.com/breathe.
- Next, do the 4-7-8 breathing exercise at www.warrior21.com/478.[38]
- Finish with two more minutes of the four-by-four breathing.

THE QUOTE THAT STARTS TODAY is powerful and incredibly mov-ing for me. I was first inspired by the importance of the semicolon during my suicide-prevention work. The wonderful Project Semicolon[39] reminds anyone struggling (including having thoughts of suicide) to stop and pause. You matter.

The semicolon reminds us to stop and pause, to practice our breathing to help ground us. Here on day 6, remember you are not on this journey alone. There are others who did it before, people doing it now in your cohort, and more will follow. Pausing can help you gather your perspective to bring calm, focus, and inner strength, showing that you have come far already.

You are at day 6. Today's writing is intended to continue building and enhancing your practice. The only way to improve and create new habits is by pausing and dedicating the time to actually do it. It takes more than just one or two days; that's why this program is twenty-one days.

When we stop and pause, we can learn. Learning occurs not just from directly practicing something; we can become better at something through observation. Gilkey and Kilts share more:

Traditionally, scientists have assumed that people gain new skills through practice—that is through direct experience—but the existence of mirror neurons means you can also gain skills through observation and indirect experience.[40]

Pausing slows things down to allow you to think about your core beliefs. Famous psychologist Judith S. Beck, as shared by Dr. Seth Gillihan, explains core beliefs:

[Core beliefs are] the most fundamental level of belief; they are global, rigid, and overgeneralized.[41]

Gillihan then further explains:

> In other words, core beliefs form the bed-
> rock of how we see the world.[42]

Pausing to stop and collect your thoughts can help you focus on your core beliefs and then let you focus on making sure your actions are consistent with them. Pausing also helps you reflect on the cognitive triangle (day 2) and ensures the thoughts you are having are both beneficial and accurate. Accept two things: you don't have control over everything going on around you, but you do have control over yourself and how you will handle it.

Dr. Rick Hanson adds more:

> Life is turbulent and unpredictable, contain-
> ing wonderful opportunities that still take a
> lot of work and inevitable losses and pains.
> We can't avoid challenges. The only ques-
> tion is how we deal with them.
>
> There is a fundamental difference between
> facing challenges while experiencing that
> your needs are being sufficiently met, and
> facing challenges while experiencing that
> your needs are *not* being met. ...
>
> A deepening awareness of your wants and
> needs—and your thoughts and feelings
> *about* them—can help you meet them more
> effectively and accept yourself more fully.[43]

When you pause, it gives you time to check in with yourself to make sure you're looking out for and taking care of yourself. Again, that's not selfish. It is smart and expected. Pausing helps you work toward achieving your goals, and it also helps you help others.

As mentioned above, the use of the semicolon is inspired by Project Semicolon,[44] a suicide-prevention group.

With the **warr;or21** concept, the semicolon takes on a different meaning. Today and every day, pause, stop, reflect, and start with the breath. This allows you to assess your thoughts, your feelings and emotions, and your actions.

Reflection

How do you feel, knowing about the impact of the semicolon and that you are now part of the positive movement behind it?

Try to do the 4-7-8 breathing exercise a second time at some point during the day (sitting down if you need to).

Take a minute and share your perspective with someone on how things are going with your **warr;or21** journey. Write down in your notebook, on the back, left-side page, one thing you have enjoyed about the **warr;or21** program, one thing that has surprised you so far, and the most challenging part so far. If you want to, share this on social media using the #warrior21days tag.

Now that you have identified the most challenging part, you can prepare yourself for next time if it comes up. Instead of it being a roadblock, you can develop a plan to deal with it and also utilize your resilience practices such as controlled breathing.

Evening Practice

In your notebook, write down answers to the following, and remember not to repeat your previous answers:

1. One thing that made you happy today
2. One nice thing someone did for you today
3. One nice thing you did for someone today

Take a moment after you write these down and then go back and review the previous five days. Notice how you haven't repeated yourself. This is growth, and it builds resilience. Don't overlook the importance of this; instead, think about how much you have already accomplished by doing this practice each evening. Well done. That's impressive.

Day 7: Practice

We are what we repeatedly do. Excellence
then, is not an act but a habit.
—Will Durant

Morning Breathing Practice

- As early as possible after you wake up, dedicate five minutes to breathing to help you get focused for the day and realize that you are setting your perspective.
- Start off with one minute of four-by-four breathing (four seconds inhaling and four seconds exhaling). Remember, you can use the animated shield graphic here if you need to: https://www.warrior21.com/breathe.
- Next, do the 4-7-8 breathing exercise at www.warrior21.com/478.[45]
- Finish with two more minutes of breathing four seconds in and four seconds out.

  o Remember, this is rewiring your brain and creating new habits that will stick.

    ▪ Before you begin, tell yourself you are choosing to do it and tell yourself why you are doing it. Remind yourself you are doing this because you are choosing to look after your mental health and build your resilience.

- As you are doing it, enjoy it—connect it with being positive. This is important.
- When you finish, take a brief moment to reflect on what you just accomplished because you chose to do it.

TO BE GREAT AT SOMETHING, there is no way around hard work and practice—lots of practice. It's been said that it takes ten thousand hours to be an expert at something. The truth behind that statement is that it must be done with dedicated purposed. Practice with intent, with purpose—every single time. Avoid half-efforted attempts or moving along robotically. The intensity is grueling. So, how do you stick with it? You must also enjoy what you are practicing. That is critical.

Seriously, take a moment and read that first paragraph again. This is the neuroscience behind rewiring your brain to have greater resilience and improve your mental health. It is not just about doing it but also knowingly making the choice, wanting to, and enjoying it.

In a famous Arnold Schwarzenegger video,[46] he mentions that when someone asked him why he smiled often at the gym, he replied he enjoyed being there. He added that it did not make lifting heavier weights any easier, but he enjoyed it. He worked out for five hours a day … after working in construction all day.

He wanted to do it. He accepted the challenge and knew how it would help him while he also enjoyed it. This sounds like having a passion and perseverance (grit, day 4).

In another segment, he refers to a famous Muhammad Ali quote that he uses for inspiration to keep practicing with intensity. Someone asked Ali how many sit-ups he did. His answer was that he did not start counting until it hurt. Practice builds grit and develops resilience. Our positive outlook reminds us to enjoy the journey. Sounds just like what we are doing for **warr;or21**, right?

For those who enjoy physical fitness activities, think of this **warr;or21** journey as mental workouts. Much like physical activities, such as running, CrossFit, HIIT, squats, bench presses, and pull-ups, develop muscles, this journey builds mental muscles.

This type of cognitive fitness, as described by Gilkey and Kilts, helps you handle life's stressors and tough situations:

> The more cognitively fit you are, the better you will be able to make decisions, solve problems, and deal with stress and change.
>
> Cognitive fitness will allow you to be more open to new ideas and alternative perspectives. It will give you the capacity to change your behaviors and forecast their outcomes in order to realize your goals.[47]

Let the above passage serve as a reminder that it is not just physical fitness that keeps you healthy. Cognitive fitness is critical to being good at anything you do. It helps you develop new positive habits and, importantly, gives you the mental strength to stick with them.

When you practice with purpose, you realize that "practice makes perfect" means things will not go perfectly during your practice; you will experience setbacks and failures. It is with grit (day 4) and perspective (day 16) that you learn from setbacks and failures to move forward. Angela Duckworth, an expert on grit, explains:

When you look at people practicing, you find they make tons and tons of mistakes. It's by making those mistakes that you get better. Making mistakes and failing are normal—in fact, they're necessary.[48]

Duckworth goes on to share that there is no way around practice, and it is not easy.

Getting anywhere in life, doing anything worth doing, it just takes so much effort.

If things were easier, then maybe we wouldn't need grit. But I think most things that are worth doing take a long time and that sustained commitment. There are no shortcuts to true excellence.[49]

This isn't about sugarcoating things. It takes effort to be good at something, yet when it is a passion of yours, like your mental health and increasing resilience, it makes it worth persevering. With passion for what you are doing (like this program), you can make the decision to practice, to constantly strive to get better. You're making a great choice by continuing the **warr;or** journey.

Reflection

Consider where you are in life right now. Reflect on how your practice and dedication have gotten you to where you are. It certainly required sacrifice. Reflecting on the sacrifice is not about having a one-person pity party. You made the choice—own it and be happy with it. Your success is due to your actions.

No matter who you are and what type of successes you have, stay hungry.

Stay passionate. Check in with yourself today to make sure you are truly still pushing yourself. Make sure you are enjoying it too. Take twelve minutes today to click the Arnold video (see citation #46) and watch the twelve minutes straight. You'll thank me later.

Finally, share your perspective on this with someone today. Do it. Don't skip this.

Evening Practice

In your notebook, write down answers to the following questions, remembering not to repeat your previous responses:

1. One thing that made you happy today
2. One nice thing someone did for you today
3. One nice thing you did for someone today

For tonight's gratitude practice, consider trying to include someone else. See what they think about participating in it. Ask them to try it, even if it sounds odd or silly. Let them know how it has been going for you now that you are in your seventh day of practicing it.

Day 8: Resilience

Persistence and resilience only come from having been given the chance to work through difficult problems.
—Gever Tulley

Morning Breathing Practice

- As early as possible after you wake up, dedicate five minutes to breathing to help you get focused for the day and realize that you are setting your perspective.
- Start off with one minute of four-by-four breathing (four seconds inhaling and four seconds exhaling). Remember, you can use the animated shield graphic here if you need to: https://www. warrior21.com/breathe.
- Next, do the 4-7-8 breathing exercise.[50]
- Finish with two more minutes of four-by-four breathing (four seconds in and four seconds out).
- Yep, the same breathing practices are three days in a row. This is building resilience. Stick with it, find your grit and your calm, and add a bit of gratitude, realizing the purpose of it. You are creating new, strong, positive practices, and this is the foundation of resilience.

RESILIENCE, ALONG WITH POSITIVE MENTAL health, is at the core of **warr;or21**. Each is part of every single practice, every single day.

Day 8 though is dedicated to *resilience*, allowing you to reflect on the term. Everyone uses the term, so let's make sure we fully understand it.

There are a variety of definitions that for the most part all say the same thing: resilience is the ability to handle tough moments and bounce back from those adverse life events. I often tell people not to forget the second part of the definition (added by me): resilience is also about reaching out for help when needed. Inner strength is realizing that, yes, you should rely on yourself, but you should also utilize the assistance of others when needed.

Again, being resilient does not mean taking on everything alone. Nor does it mean that when you are struggling, no one will be able to help you. Resilience is the opposite of that. It gives you the strength to open up to others and be willing to let people help. Regardless of your strength, there is no reason to take it on by yourself.

Reaching out for help isn't about appealing to the person closest to you. It is strategic. Deutschendorf elaborates on this:

It's not that they [highly resilient people] never look to others for guidance and direction, it's that they are very selective in who they chose to follow. They look for mentorship in people who have achieved greatly and whom they admire. Once they have found the people they chose to follow, they soak up all the information, guidance and inspiration they can by reading their books and listening to their spoken messages for insight.[51]

Being resilient requires becoming comfortable with the uncomfortable, which includes taking calculated risks while at the same time managing impulse control. Reivich explain:

> [Resilience] means being prepared to take appropriate risk. People who score high on resilience are willing to try things and think failure is a part of life.
>
> ... Highly resilient people are able to tolerate ambiguity so they don't rush to make decisions. They sit back and look at things in a thoughtful way before acting.[52]

Margolis and Stoltz explain that being resilient requires pausing and focusing before acting:

> Independent studies and our own observations suggest that the ability to bounce back from adversity hinges on uncovering and untangling one's implicit beliefs about it—and shifting how one responds.[53]

Linda Graham, MFT, elaborates:

> To cope with change, we have to change how we cope. No matter the external trigger, it's our internal response, based on our neural wiring, that's important for resilience.[54]

Margolis and Stoltz further add that numerous research studies connect resilience with the perception of control:

> Our reactions to stressful situations depend on the degree of control we can exercise.[55]

Resilience, as discussed above, is not just being determined. There is clearly another important aspect to it: the response is thought out, controlled, and purposeful. Having resilience means knowing what you can't control and ensuring that you are strategic with what you can control.

Dr. Rick Hanson reminds us of an important term connected to resilience—agency. He explains:

> Agency is the sense of being a *cause* rather than the effect. Agency is present if you deliberately pick the blue sweater over a red one or listen to someone express an opinion and think, "Nah, I don't agree with that." With agency, you are active rather than passive, taking initiative and directing your life rather than being swept along.

> Agency is central to grit ... if you've been knocked down by life, agency is the first thing you draw on to get up off the floor.[56]

> Agency is the opposite of helplessness.[57]

> It typically takes many experiences of agency to compensate for a single experience of

helplessness, another example of the brain's negativity bias. To prevent helplessness in the first place or to gradually unlearn it, look for experiences in which you are making a choice or influencing an outcome.

Then focus on and take into yourself the sense of being an active agent: a hammer rather than the nail.[58]

Be the hammer—not the nail. That's some powerful stuff right there!

Finally, with respect to the **warr;or21** version of resilience, there are four pillars:

1. **Awareness:** Our thoughts, emotions, and feelings, as well as our behavior (reread day 2 if you need a refresher). Additionally, awareness (and control) of our breathing.
2. **Wellness:** Both our mental and physical health.
3. **Purpose:** Having individual goals and goals that serve others.
4. **Positivity:** An outlook grounded in realistic optimism and connecting with those close to us.

Although the introduction mentioned each, *resilience* being the keyword reminds us how important each is. Although life can be like a hurricane or tumultuous seas knocking you around as you try to tread water, the above four are like four pillars of a buoy. You need to avoid treading for too long or going too far from them. Constantly checking in with each gives us the energy to persevere.

Reflection

After reading the above, think about how you have been practicing these four resiliency skills your entire life and how, with **warr;or21**, you have been enhancing them in many different ways.

There are some especially great quotes today. Think about one that stands out for you.

At some point today, reflect on the fact that you are at day 8. You have been doing this for more than a week now. Write down three words in your notebook to describe how you feel about where you are now. Share those three words on social media (if you want), using the #warrior21days tag.

Evening Practice

In your notebook, write down answers to the following questions, remembering not to repeat your previous responses:

1. One thing that made you happy today
2. One nice thing someone did for you today
3. One nice thing you did for someone today

Day 9: Wisdom

Lessons in life will be repeated until they are learned.
—Frank Sonnenberg

Morning Breathing Practice

- As early as possible after you wake up, dedicate five minutes to breathing to help you get focused for the day and realize that you are setting your perspective.
- Start off with one minute of four-by-four breathing (four seconds inhaling and four seconds exhaling). Remember, you can use the animated shield graphic here if you need to: https://www.warrior21.com/breathe.
- Next, do the 4-7-8 breathing exercise.[59]
- Now let's try something new: guided imagery with our breathing. Think of a favorite place you enjoy going to. Shortly, you will close your eyes and picture it. As you do, experience it with your senses.

  o What are four things you see?
  o What are three different things you can touch? What does each feel like?
  o What are two different things you can hear?
  o What is one thing you can smell?
  o Finally, describe how you feel while experiencing this.

LET'S FACE IT. TODAY'S KEYWORD is something that is not guaranteed even if you do practice (day 7) continually. Your practice allows you to prepare for situations, and your wisdom allows you to adapt when things do not go as planned or happen unexpectedly. With respect to yesterday's discussion on resilience (day 8), possessing wisdom gives you intelligent resilience instead of a *never give up* attitude of simply (and foolishly) continually to do the same thing and expecting different results (yes, that is based on an Einstein quote).

Wisdom is a combination of your life experiences and your education. Your education is not limited to school but includes what you learn from all situations, reflecting on your thinking, emotions, feelings, and actions (day 2). Wisdom needs experience, yet having experiences does not automatically give you wisdom. Similarly, practicing does not guarantee possessing an expertise.

Dr. Leah Weiss elaborates on how gaining wisdom comes from not just the experience itself but what we learn from it:

The process hinges on committing to a learning mindset, experimenting, seeking feedback, paying attention to emotions, and then reflecting to absorb lessons from the experience.[60]

A key to wisdom is taking the time to stop (pause), reflect, and discern things. Note, discern does not mean overanalyze. That can lead to ruminating (being consumed with repetitive negative thoughts), which can then lead to stress, anxiety, fear, and depression, among other negative results.

Weiss adds:

> The psychological trait of ruminating re-
> fers to repetitive thinking about negative
> topics (typically self-oriented) ... Unlike re-
> flection, rumination tends to focus only on
> what has gone wrong and why it is your fault.
> Rumination is reflection gone awry.[61]

Instead, the **warr;or21** type of deep reflection that leads to wisdom occurs when we calm ourselves. Yet again, this means starting with controlled breathing exercises. Controlled breathing exercises still the mind to help us see things more clearly, and when dealing with moments when we have to make difficult decisions, we are able to make the best decisions given the current situation.

You have been harnessing your wisdom and adding to it each day. The **warr;or21** program emphasizes the importance of the breathing exer- cises, but there is much more to the program than these daily exercises. Remember, as you go about each moment and day, the purpose is to increase your awareness and your mental and physical health, deepen your personal and greater purpose, and enhance your realistic optimism (being positive). This is the change you've been working on. Legitimate, long-term, and sustainable change is done by a daily practice, and you are doing it.

Before continuing, a short note on wisdom with respect to that greater purpose mentioned above—helping others. Here on day 9, take a moment to reflect on the wisdom you already have and how you are increasing it. For example, when helping others or just listening to them, ask yourself, Are you quick to pass judgment, minimize their experiences, or offer advice? Research has shown that it is not helpful to them.

Instead, think about if you are using your wisdom to help others by actively listening in a way that doesn't judge, acknowledges their emotions, and lets them know it is okay to feel what they are feeling, showing genuine interest, not making it about you or your similar experiences, and helping them figure out what is best for them to do next. By using active listening and not the other negative approaches, you are putting your wisdom in action to help others. This has numerous benefits, including for yourself.

Dr. Seth Gillihan elaborates:

> Research has shown that making a point to help others leads to improvements in anxiety and depression symptoms.[62]

Think about it. Part of increasing wisdom is gaining knowledge through experience. It is important to have someone you trust, with whom you can share your experiences and, more importantly, whose feedback you accept. Eric Barker explains more on having a mentor:

> ## 1) Find A Mentor
>
> The most important part of deliberate practice is solitary practice. Hard work. But that's not the first step.
>
> The first step is social. You need to know what to do. And that's where mentors, coaches and teachers come in. Here's [Professor] Anders:
>
> "They need to talk to somebody that they really admire, a person that is doing

something in a way that they would like to eventually be able to do. Have this person help you identify what it is that you might need to change in order to be able to do what that other person is doing.

Interview that person about how they were able to do it, and then have that person help you identify what is it that you can't do right now and what are the steps towards reaching that desired level of performance."[63]

Finally, Barker shares three tips for working toward perfection:

Once you have the knowledge, you need to focus on building the skills. Remember the three F's:

- Focus
- Feedback
- Fix it[64]

Finally, cultivating wisdom through experiences and practice can be draining. Fortunately, Nicholas Cole shares five habits to help also cultivate a positive mind-set. It includes the following:

1. **Make time for input:** This is referring to relaxing and taking time to enjoy things at an easy pace. Input modes can include reading, watching a movie, and, importantly, getting a good night's sleep.[65]

2. **Read, read, read:** Reading opens the mind, and Cole suggests you read especially in the morning, as it can serve as a type of mental exercise that gets you ready for the day:

> [Reading] is essential for constant growth. Reading is what exposes you to new ideas, teaches you things you would otherwise never have the opportunity to learn.[66]

3. **Surround yourself with positive people:** Just as being part of a gritty group is important, the group's mind-set is as well, because their positive mind-set can rub off on you.[67]

4. **Practice:** This was covered in depth yesterday and earlier today. That said, Cole reminds us about the connection between confidence, practice, and self-efficacy (believing in yourself and your abilities):

> Confidence is the result of not just doing something well, but knowing you do something well … [68]

> No amount of positive thinking can replace good habits or daily practice.[69]

5. **Find a mentor:** First, yes, Eric Barker already has covered this. That said, Cole adds:

> There is no faster and more effective way to learn in life than to find a mentor.[70]

I don't know about you, but researching and writing today's work helped me further understand what true wisdom is, and trying to practice it reminded me that regardless of age or level of expertise, we can all continue to gain wisdom—if we strive for it.

Reflection[71]

At some point today, answer the following questions in the notebook:

- What is good about me?
- If I am in a crisis, whom can I rely on to talk to (list two to three people)? What personal strengths can I rely on to help me? What strategies that have worked in the past will I be able to utilize?
- What do I value most? What actions have I taken today that are in line with what I value?

Evening Practice

In your notebook, write down answers to the following questions, remembering not to repeat your previous responses:

1. One thing that made you happy today
2. One nice thing someone did for you today
3. One nice thing you did for someone today

You have now read nine quotes. With your life's wisdom, think about your *own* quote. Imagine someone asked right now, with respect to your **warrior21** journey, "What have you learned?" What is your one-sentence reply? Write it down in quotes in your notebook. Share your quote on social media (if you'd like) and use the #warrior21days tag (trust me, people want to read it, and so do I!).

Day 10: Emotions

When you react, you let others control you.
When you respond, you are in control.
—Bodhi Sanders

Morning Breathing Practice

- As early as possible after you wake up, dedicate five minutes to breathing to help you get focused for the day and realize that you are setting your perspective.
- Start off with one minute of four-by-four breathing (four seconds inhaling and four seconds exhaling). Remember, you can use the animated shield graphic here if you need to: https://www.warrior21.com/breathe.
- Next, do the 4-7-8 breathing exercise.[72]
- Finish with two more minutes of breathing four seconds in, four seconds out.

WE ALL THINK WE UNDERSTAND emotions. Yet what if you were asked, What's the difference between emotions, moods, and feelings? Confused? Don't worry, Dr. Rick Hanson helps clarify things:

Emotions consist of feelings and moods. Feelings are specific, often fairly brief, and

> caused an inner or outer stimulus … moods
> are more diffuse, enduring, and indepen-
> dent of stimuli. Sadness is a feeling, while
> depression is a mood.[73]

The good news is that our feelings grow moods, so if we cultivate positive feelings, it then contributes to an overall positive mood. This is how resilience works; we have more control over than this we might realize.

Hanson shares the following:

> Feelings grow moods. For example, repeat-
> edly taking in feelings of gladness and grati-
> tude will tend to develop a mood of content-
> ment. In turn, moods grow feelings. A basic
> sense of contentment with life fosters feel-
> ings of thankfulness and joy. Consequently,
> taking in positive feelings can lift your mood,
> which will bring you more positive feelings,
> which can lift your mood further.[74]

This demonstrates the cyclic nature of emotions, moods, and feelings. This cycle can benefit you or it can have a negative impact on you. Guess what's a great way to ensure it is positive feelings and moods you are cultivating? Your evening practices of gratitude in your notebook. Hopefully this re-energizes you and you see how something as little as an evening practice of gratitude can have big results.

David DeSteno adds to this:

> Emotions aren't inherently bad or good;
> they're a form of mental energy. And like

any powerful force, they can be constructive or destructive depending on how they're harnessed.[75]

Having wisdom (day 9) reminds us that our interpretations of the events and situations lead to our emotions. This is important, and Dr. Leah Weiss further explains:

It is important to keep in mind that while our emotions happen in response to situations, situations don't create our emotional responses. It is the way we interpret or appraise a situation that creates our emotional response to it.[76]

The above is worth reading a second time (really, go back and read the quote again). Based on Weiss's above passage, we have to be mindful of the type of situations (and people) that can trigger certain negative emotions in us. Being aware of those emotions helps us to prepare for it and handle it. Ideally, it helps us prevent those emotions from getting out of control and dictating our actions.

Weiss adds:

When we cultivate self-awareness, we can learn our triggers and understand how to self-regulate or adapt to challenging situations ... The research consensus is that fighting against our feelings only makes them stronger ... Our brains read this as more emotion and therefore spin faster and faster until it becomes a vicious cycle and the whole dynamic intensifies. The ability to tolerate or accept or get curious about our unpleasant emotions is the ticket of this cycle.[77]

We are humans; therefore, we have emotions. I have yet to find one scientific paper that suggests we ignore our emotions. Dr. Leah Weiss has done the hard work for you and sums it up in her HBR article:

I've studied the downsides of emotional suppression … I can assure you—it's worse. It's paradoxical, but nonjudgmentally engaging with negative emotions negatively correlates with negative emotions and mood disorder.

In other words, if you acknowledge and recognize unpleasant emotions, they have less power to cause you distress.[78]

So, it's not about ignoring your emotions; it is about your perception of them. DeSteno says that there is true power in your emotions and in acknowledging them:

In truth, emotions are among the most powerful and efficient mechanisms we have to guide good decisions … The trick to success, then, comes in understanding that emotions don't happen to us; we can use them to help

achieve our goals—if we develop the wisdom to call upon the right emotions to meet
the challenges at hand.[79]

Additionally, certain emotions can be helpful to your success. DeSteno
explains:

When it comes to long-term success, the
"right" emotions are principally these: gratitude, compassion, and pride. These emotions, unlike basic feelings of happiness,
sadness, anger, or fear, are intrinsically tied
to social life, and that provides the key to
their effectiveness.[80]

And here, Southwick and Charney further explain the benefits of these
types of positive emotions:

Positive emotions, in contrast [to negative
emotions], have been shown to reduce physiological arousal and to broaden our visual
focus, thoughts, and our behavior. When people experience positive emotions and an ac-
companying broadening of attention and behavior, their thinking tends to become more
creative, inclusive, flexible, and integrative.[81]

Emotional regulation, control, and acknowledgment allows us to account
for our emotions to ensure they do not dictate our actions and lead us
to out-of-control behavior that we most likely will regret later on (if not
immediately).

When helping other people going through a crisis or tough time, acknowledging their emotions after you have control of your own can help that person gain (or regain) a more rational approach to whatever issues they might be experiencing. This helps them focus and determine how best to approach their situation while also being open to your ideas and suggestions. Being able to effectively do this is the backbone of active listening skills used by experts, including hostage negotiators[82] and crisis counselors.[83]

Looking back on day 2, part of the cognitive triangle entails accounting for our emotions. This truly is a work in progress, and we all know from our personal life experiences there is definitely not a finish line to this. Yet again, our breathing practices are directly connected to our emotions and trying to control and manage them.

For the untrained person though, it can be hard to realize that practicing breathing daily can help us in heated, emotionally charged moments. Yet Dr. Alex Korb reminds us:

Changing your breathing is a powerful tool ... because it is one of the quickest ways to change your emotional state.[84]

You are now nearly halfway into **warr;or21**, and I am pretty certain you, after practicing this for ten days, are starting to realize what Dr. Korb just shared above.

Reflection

Take a moment to think about a key aspect of the article that means a lot to you. How will it impact how you go about the rest of your day? Write one keyword that comes to mind after doing this on the next blank, right-side page in your notebook for day 10.

At some point today, do the following exercise (or save it for the weekend). On the blank, opposite, left side of the page you just wrote on for day 10, draw the tip of an iceberg, then a squiggly line for water, and then a big portion of the iceberg below it. On the tip of the iceberg, write "happy" inside it.

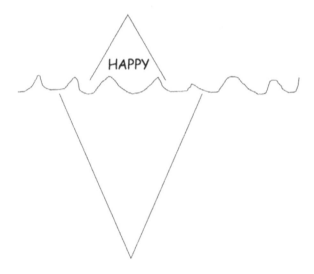

Think of the last time you felt happy.

Obviously, you were happy, but now dig deeper and go below the surface. Why did you feel so happy? What was it about the situation that made you so happy? Write inside the bottom part of the iceberg three to five corresponding emotions that further elaborate why you felt happy.

Doing this exercise will help you reflect again and longer on a happy moment and thus further rewire your brain to recall and stay with happy moments. This is how building resilience and enhancing your mental health works. You read about positive emotions earlier today.

Additionally, by looking deeper into the other emotions connected with this moment, you are understanding more deeply your emotions other than just *happy*.

By doing this, you are better able to understand your emotions, yet it doesn't stop with you. When you further understand your emotions, it helps you understand other people's emotions and their experiences. This increased your empathy.

Finally, today at some point, start a conversation with someone to share your thoughts on today's keyword or the iceberg exercise. Get their input too.

Evening Practice

In your notebook, write down answers to the following questions, remembering not to repeat your previous responses:

1. One thing that made you happy today
2. One nice thing someone did for you today
3. One nice thing you did for someone today

Day 11: Reflection

> With reflection, we can create a stronger relation-
> ship to our experience than our usual partial, biased,
> semiconscious one. When we consider something
> deeply, and with precision, we see it more clearly.
> —Leah Weiss, PhD

Morning Breathing Practice

- As early as possible after you wake up, dedicate five minutes to breathing to help you get focused for the day and realize that you are setting your perspective.
- Start off with one minute of four-by-four breathing (four seconds inhaling and four seconds exhaling). Remember, you can use the animated shield graphic here if you need to: https://www.warrior21.com/breathe.
- Next, do two minutes of guided breathing. As you breathe in, say to yourself, "I am strong." As you breathe out, say to yourself, "I am calm."
- Finally, do the 4-7-8 breathing exercise.[85]

NOW THAT YOUR JOURNEY IS at the halfway point, today is a great opportunity to pause and reflect.

You surely are not the same person you were when you started.

You are halfway through this warrior path. It is not to become some sort of soldier in the midst of a war, fighting for your life. Instead, the **warr;or** path you are on is an internal one that is filled with grit, resilience, wisdom, and a sense of calmness that projects a greater sense of professionalism in what you do. Overall, this is your inner strength, and you have been increasing it.

You are not only building resilience and inner strength; you are also taking care of your mental health. That is true strength. This is what makes you effective at helping others.

The only way for this to happen is by looking out for yourself first. Understanding the connection between your thoughts, emotions, feelings, and behaviors (day 2) gives you a deeper perspective on how to control what you can and accept those things that are beyond your control. Even in those circumstances, your perspective on control reminds you that you still control yourself and how you respond. That is powerful. That is about understanding perspective, and this is how you have been rewiring your brain over the past ten days.

Your daily breathing practices enhance your control over your thinking, emotions, feelings, and behavior, while the evening gratitude practices remind you that your reality is shaped by your perspective—a perspective that you have a choice in defining, a perspective you have been managing and enhancing. This deepens your personal purpose and further contributes to seeing how you are serving a greater purpose beyond yourself. It is also helping you achieve the goals you wrote down in the front of your notebook.

Dr. Jeremy Dean reminds us of how purpose is connected to happiness:

Feeling useful and having a sense of purpose
in life are clearly beneficial psychologically,

but now research is revealing that there also physical benefits.

No matter what your age, new research finds, having a sense of purpose helps you live longer.[86]

Today's keyword, *reflection*, allows you to be honest with yourself. Have you done all of the practices each day? Have you put 100 percent into all of it? If not, use this this time to check in with yourself and recharge.

Weiss's quote to start today demonstrates that the act of reflecting is not a quick and simple process. It takes work and effort.

Ask yourself, Are you challenging yourself enough? We already discussed that regarding this program, so let's move beyond that. Are you eating healthy enough? Are you getting enough sleep? Are you working out hard enough? Are you making sure you spend time with family and friends?

Only you know the answers, and without pausing to reflect, you can fall into mediocrity, and that is not you. If it were, you wouldn't be reading this. Be honest with yourself and keep pushing yourself. Do it. Challenge yourself. Smile at the challenges (day 17, by the way, is "Smile") and embrace them not because it will be easy but because you are making the choice. Growth occurs when you are out of your comfort zone.

Reflection is more than just reviewing. Reflection is analyzing, discerning (looking deeply), and not being overly critical of one's self. Reflection is allowing yourself to pause to make sure you understand situations and events accurately and not in a distorted way. This leads to wisdom (day 9). Go back and look at day 2. Read it again, and now with your added days of experience and wisdom, it can be much more profound and meaningful.

Again though, don't use this time to be hard on yourself. Dr. Alex Korb emphasizes this and how it's not helpful. He also adds a bit of neuroscience to the mix:

Often when we try to start a good habit and then slip up, we describe it as a failure of willpower. But sticking to a good habit is simply a matter of willpower. You have will-power only insofar as your prefrontal cortex is paying attention and has enough sero-tonin to work properly.[87]

Getting upset with yourself does not help the process of retraining the brain. It hin-ders it. Those feelings of frustration or self-judgement are all sources of stress, making it more likely that you'll keep doing your old habits.[88]

Keep in mind, although you want to continually push yourself, you also want to do it in a supportive way. Be your number one supporter, not your number one enemy, constantly being overly critical and negative about yourself.

Dr. Kristin Neff describes this as having self-compassion (note, it is not self-esteem, as many would think). Self-compassion helps you to be fair with yourself and avoid being endlessly self-critical, which can push you deeper into a downward spiral of self-negativity. Instead, Neff explains:

Self-compassion honors the fact that all human beings have both strengths and

weaknesses … we feel more connected …
self-compassion is associated with signifi-
cantly less anxiety and depression, as well
as more happiness, optimism, and positive
emotions.[89]

Remember, your grittiness pushes you forward, your wisdom tells you how to do it, and your patience (with yourself) allows you the time to do it. Don't forget to enjoy the journey too.

Reflecting can help you focus on how to move forward. This is accomplished by setting goals, specifically small goals—really small goals. Dr. Sean Young recommends (backed by research) having steps (what you can do right now), short-term goals (achievable within a week), long-term goals (within the month), and dreams (three months or more). His stepladder process connects each of those. Young explains further:

Science shows that people have a better
chance of success by focusing on small
steps. Yet even when they know this, people repeatedly fail to make changes last.
That's because they don't understand just
how small those steps need to be and don't
have a model to guide them.[90]

You need to focus on completing small,
concrete goals to calibrate the mind and
apply stepladders correctly. That will make
change more likely to last … stepladders
isn't a formula for accomplishing dreams.
It's a formula for keeping you on the path.[91]

After reflecting on how far you have come on this **warr;or** journey, you get to make the decision to keep moving forward. This is the way. Onward, **warr;or**.

Simply making a decision reduces stress. You're controlling what you can. That helps you handle and manage those things that are beyond your control.

Korb explains:

> You don't even need direct control over the cause of your stress to gain benefits of decision making. As long as you have control over something, you can take advantage of the benefits.[92]

> The important thing here is not actual control, but perceived control. Making decisions may not increase your actual control over a situation, but it will likely increase your perceived control. And when you increase your perceived control, you increase your confidence, mood, and future decision-making capabilities.[93]

Korb eloquently explains how resilience and positive mental health are doable. We have the tools at our disposal.

The best part about all of this is there is still more to go—more days of practice, more nights of gratitude. Again, remember how the gritty person (you!) sees things. In front of you are the challenges, and they continue. You got yourself to this point, and your reward is getting to keep going forward. You just have to make the decision to do it.

Reflection

At some point today, have a look back at your notebook. Reflect, without judgment, on all the hard work you have already done. It was not easy, and there were most likely moments when you felt like taking a break or quitting, but your resilience and determination kept you going. Even if there was a moment, or day, you didn't meet all of the requirements, that is okay too. You got back at it, and you made it here. See that as a challenge you accepted and surpassed.

Reflect on one key point from the above explanation of today's keyword and how it can help motivate you going forward, during the remaining days and beyond this twenty-one-day journey. Try to have a conversation with someone about it too.

Finally, ever hear someone say to another person, usually during an argument or disagreement, in an accusatory manner, "You did that on purpose!"?

Now, take that same saying, which is often said in a negative manner, and flip it. With your **warr;or** perspective and ability to reflect, use that same saying to encourage yourself. Tell yourself the next time you do something positive (the breathing exercise, pausing during the day, the evening gratitude practice, etc.), "You did this on purpose!"

I recommend saying it internally and not out loud. That might sound weird if others are around, as you'll be talking to yourself!

Know that using positive words of encouragement directed at you is part of rewiring your brain to build inner strength—and yep, you guessed it, it is backed by research.

Onward, **warr;or**!

Evening Practice

In your notebook, write down answers to the following questions, remembering not to repeat your previous responses:

1. One thing that made you happy today
2. One nice thing someone did for you today
3. One nice thing you did for someone today

Day 12: Stress

Adapting the right attitude can convert a negative stress into a positive one.
—Hans Selye

Morning Breathing Practice

- As early as possible after you wake up, dedicate five minutes to breathing to help you get focused for the day and realize that you are setting your perspective.
- Start off with four minutes of four-by-four breathing (four seconds inhaling and four seconds exhaling). Remember, you can use the animated shield graphic here if you need to: https://www.warrior21.com/breathe.
- Next, do two minutes of guided breathing. As you breathe in, say to yourself, "I am strong." As you breathe out, say to yourself, "I am calm."
- Next, do the 4-7-8 breathing exercise.[94]

STRESS IS PART OF LIVING regardless of your employment or if you are a student. Likewise, having anxiety from time to time is also normal. Both stress and anxiety become a cause for concern when they begin to interfere with our cognitive and behavioral functioning and have a detrimental impact on our mood. Stress can then become inhibiting, and our anxiety can become irrational.

When unchecked and prolonged, the negative impact of stress includes the following:[95]

Physical	Mood	Behavior
headaches	anxiety	over/undereating
muscle tension/pain	restlessness	angry outburst
chest pain	lack of motivation or focus	drug/alcohol misuse
fatigue	feeling overwhelmed	tobacco use
change in sex drive	irritability or anger	social withdrawal
upset stomach	sadness or depression	exercising less often
sleep problems		

Stress can be caused by the situations you are involved in and your perception regarding the concept of control. The key to handling stress is how you embrace the situation. You might not have asked for the situation, but you do control your response and the way you think about it. You can choose to either handle it or let it overwhelm you.

Alia and Thomas Crum acknowledge that long-term stress can take a negative toll, yet they also share how stress can be positive, as it shows we care about something and can lead to personal growth.[96]

The two Crums' work and research on executives, students, and Navy SEALs regarding handling stress resulted in a three-step process: 1) see it, 2) own it, and 3) use it. Each are explained more below:

1) **See It**

Rather than denying it, or dwelling upon it, we recommend simply naming or labeling the stress you are facing ... [97]

2) Own It

Stress shows us that we care; that the stakes matter. Owning this realization unleashes positive motivation—because deep down we know that things that are important shouldn't always come easy.[98]

3) Use It

The issue, then, is not in the stress response itself but in how we channel or employ this response. Simply reframing your response to stress as something that is beneficial can be helpful. [99]

Anxiety can also be used to your advantage. Alicia Clarke states that it can actually be "pathway to our best selves." She first cautions:

To be sure, severe anxiety can be debilitating. But for many people who experience it at more moderate levels it can be helpful, if we are open enough to embrace and reframe it.[100]

Clarke continues explaining that it is our perspective on anxiety and stress that can shape our reality:

How we think about anxiety and stress can change how those feelings impact us. Regardless of actual stress levels, the less harmful you believe the feeling is, the less harmful it will be.[101]

Clarke then quotes Alia Crum (yes, the same Alia Crum I quoted earlier):

"Our minds actually change reality. In other words the reality we will experience tomorrow is in part a product of the mind-sets we hold today."[102]

Clarke provides tips on harnessing anxiety to your benefit. One tip is this:

Naming anxiety—and then renaming it—allows you to process its message rather than just react to its discomfort. This reduces distress and activates better emotional regulation, problem solving and planning.[103]

Of course, one other way to help us manage stress and our anxiety when both arise is controlled breathing exercises. Dr. Alex Korb reminds us of how important controlled breathing is:

Changing your breathing is a powerful tool for creating an upward spiral, because it is one of the quickest ways to change your emotional state.[104]

Breathing affects the brain through the vagus nerve. Not only does the vagus nerve send signals down to the heart ... it also carries up into the brain stem. Vagus nerve signaling is important in activating circuits for resting and relaxation.[105]

If stress and anxiety can be useful, then learning more about the positive approaches to each only makes sense. Click the above highlighted links to take a deeper dive into understanding each if you'd like. You still might be wondering about long-term stressful situations and ones that you can't get out of, such as family conflicts and work environments. Don't stress (pun intended), as Crum and Crum address that too, especially because it is not always clear how to use the stress:

The key in these cases is to simply be open to the opportunities and learning inherent in the stress.[106]

Admittedly, when I first read the above passage, I was still left with questions. Fortunately, Crum and Crum answered them with their final sentence of the article by clarifying that they don't suggest that all stressors are positive:

But we do advocate that you embrace your stress response as a powerful tool for helping you overcome the inevitable challenges in life that can—and will—arise.[107]

Today's article and information on stress can guide you the next time you experience stress and anxiety, as you have new tools (and old ones like controlled breathing) to guide you through it in a positive way.

Reflection

If you feel stress today, reflect on how your breathing practices for the past twelve days have prepared you to handle it. Really.

Also, consider how you have already implemented many of the tips offered in the articles. That's an accomplishment, and you should pause to acknowledge that. Congratulate yourself because you have been doing this—and you have been doing it on purpose. Reflect on how you can better utilize some of the tips in the article today and moving forward.

Pick a close friend or family member and share this perspective on stress and anxiety, and if you're up for it, talk about the vagus nerve!

Evening Practice

In your notebook, write down answers to the following questions, remembering not to repeat your previous responses:

1. One thing that made you happy today
2. One nice thing someone did for you today
3. One nice thing you did for someone today

Day 13: Empathy

Empathy is produced not only by how we perceive information, but also how we understand that information, are moved by it, and use it to motivate our behavior.
—Dr. Helen Riess

Morning Breathing Practice

- As early as possible after you wake up, dedicate five minutes to breathing to help you get focused for the day and realize that you are setting your perspective.
- Start off with one minute of four-by-four breathing (four seconds inhaling and four seconds exhaling). Remember, you can use the animated shield graphic here if you need to: https://www.warrior21.com/breathe.
- Next, do the 4-7-8 breathing exercise.[108]
- Now let's do guided imagery with our breathing. Think of a favorite place you enjoy going to. Shortly, you will close your eyes, picturing it. As you do, experience it with your senses.

  o What are four things you see?
  o What are three different things you can touch? What does each feel like?
  o What are two different things you can hear?

o   What is one thing you can smell?

o   Finally, describe how you feel while experiencing this.

EMPATHY IS ARGUABLY ONE OF the most important words in the world, and it is too important to be limited to this ink on paper (or digital ink if you're reading this on an electronic device). Empathy is not sympathy (we'll discuss sympathy tomorrow, day 14). Empathy is understanding another person's perspective, their actions, and what they are feeling. Sympathy moves beyond empathy in that it entails feeling compassion for the person who is struggling, in crisis, or having a hard time. Both empathy and sympathy can be used to motivate a person to help others.

Empathy is strategic. From that perspective, it is one of the most important tools in a law enforcement officer's toolbox (remember, this program was originally designed for law enforcement). If the officer is involved in an incident where they need to get someone to do what they want, that often means they also need the person to first stop doing what they are doing.

Empathy (and common sense) tell us that it makes it much easier for the officer to gain the person's voluntary compliance through a behavioral change if the officer understands why the person is doing what they are doing and why they are refusing (if that is the case) to do what the officer is asking them to do.

Empathy gives you insight into their current thinking, emotions, feelings, and behaviors (yep, that's exactly what day 2 is, and this is connecting the dots by demonstrating how each day is connected to other days).

When you have empathy and a greater understanding of a person's perspective, feelings, and actions, it allows you to develop a realistic strategy as you seek to influence them in a positive manner to get them to start doing what you want them to do. This way, you both win.

Let me be clear. This goes beyond the law enforcement world and applies to each and every one us and our daily actions. We are constantly seeking to influence others, and having empathy makes it easier.

The foundation for gaining an understanding of a person's thinking, emotions, feelings, and behaviors is active listening. Fortunately for all of us, Dr. Helen Riess, founder of Empathetics, Inc., wrote the book on it. She shares her insights about harnessing empathy and provides practical tips.[109]

Before we get to her tips, Justin Bariso's article explains how Daniel Goleman and Paul Eckman's work details the different types of empathy:

Cognitive empathy is the ability to understand how a person feels and what they might be thinking. Cognitive empathy makes us better communicators, because it helps us relay information in a way that best reaches the other person.

Emotional empathy (also known as affective empathy) is the ability to share the feelings of another person. Some have described it as "your pain in my heart." This type of empathy helps you build emotional connections with others.

Compassionate empathy (also known as empathic concern) goes beyond simply understanding others and sharing their feelings: it actually moves us to take action, to help however we can.[110]

In Riess's book, she offers her EMPATHY acronym to ensure we are paying attention to various actions that can help us demonstrate empathy. The explanations below are from Julie Suttie's article on Riess's work:

- **Eye contact.** An appropriate level of eye contact makes people feel seen and improves effective communication.

- **Muscles in facial expressions.** ... By being able to identify another's feelings—often by distinctive facial muscle patterns—and mirroring them, we can help communicate empathy.

- **Posture.** ... By understanding what postures communicate, we can take a more open posture—face forward, legs and arms uncrossed, leaning toward someone—to encourage more open communication and trust.

- **Affect (or emotions).** Learning to identify what another is feeling and naming it can help us better understand their behavior or the message behind their words.

- **Tone.**

- **Hearing.** ... Empathic listening means asking questions that help people

express what's really going on and listening without judgment.

- **Your response.** Riess is not talking about
what you'll say next, but how you reso-
nate with the person you are talking to. [111]

Riess explains that the benefits of cultivating empathy starts with you as
an individual, yet it moves beyond that:

Nourishing empathy lets us help not just
ourselves, but also everyone we interact
with, whether for a moment or a lifetime. [112]

Dr. Emma Seppälä details various nonverbal communication cues that
are important to empathy and trust building. Two of them, attention and
authenticity, are detailed below:

Attention. Our mind wanders 50 percent of
the time, research suggests. Moreover, given
our busy schedules and the messages and
emails that are popping onto our screens
throughout the day, we sometimes are not
present with the people in front of us—we're
still processing something that happened
earlier, or we're thinking about an article we
just read or a phone conversation we just
had. And the people you are talking to can
tell. Because you are not fully present, you
are less likely to hear them and respond to

them skillfully, let alone understand where they are coming from.

Authenticity. Despite all this advice, it's critical that you be authentic, or your efforts will backfire. Just think of how you feel when you're around someone who seems to be something they are not: We often walk away feeling uncomfortable or manipulated. Our blood pressure rises in the face of inauthenticity, according to research by James Gross at Stanford University.[113]

Today's information provides practical tips and actions to be mindful of when attempting to demonstrate empathy. We can all apply these tips in our lives, regardless of what we do for a living.

As a reminder, don't forget this **warr;or21** journey is only twenty-one days. It is designed to help you create new positive habits to help yourself and others beyond these twenty-one days of practice. That is the meaning of having both purpose and empathy. It is not solely for personal gains. True empathy, as Dr. Riess would agree, is also about creating the best positive outcomes for others as well.

From that perspective, consider reading more on active listening skills[114] and taking courses such as Mental Health First Aid,[115] where you can gain a greater understanding of mental health and conditions, suicide prevention, and how to engage someone who might be in a crisis. Consider taking it a step further and volunteer for a great organization, such as Crisis Text Line.[116]

Reflection

Today, take some time to really listen to someone. As the readings show and Dr. Riess's quote demonstrates, there is a lot to empathy. Active listening is a critical part. Let people close to you know that they matter today by giving them your attention and care by demonstrating empathy. Be guided by the tips shared today. Tip one: put the mobile phone down while they are talking!

Evening Practice

In your notebook, write down answers to the following questions, remembering not to repeat your previous responses:

1. One thing that made you happy today.
2. One nice thing someone did for you today.
3. One nice thing you did for someone today.
4. Similar to day 6, write down how you feel about doing this program and making it to the end of day 13. Also write down what the best part of the program is so far for you. Next, go back to day 6 and compare it to that.

Day 14: Sympathy

> If you want to take care of other people, you
> simply cannot do so effectively if you are
> not taking adequate care of yourself.
> —Dan Harris

Morning Breathing Practice

- As early as possible after you wake up, dedicate five minutes to breathing to help you get focused for the day and realize that you are setting your perspective.
- Start off with four minutes of four-by-four breathing (four seconds inhaling and four seconds exhaling). Remember, you can use the animated shield graphic here if you need to: https://www.warrior21.com/breathe.
- Next, do the 4-7-8 breathing exercise.[117]

SYMPATHY IS A NATURAL RESPONSE when wanting to help others. Why? Well, your motivation to help others most likely involves assisting those who are stressed, confused, or in a personal crisis. It is normal to feel bad for someone going through a tough moment, to have compassion for them and to want to assist however you can. Our brains are wired to have sympathy (also empathy), and there is lots of research to back that up.[118]

With sympathy (and also with empathy), we have to look out for ourselves first. If we are constantly striving to help others, a necessary first step is self-care. Think about it. A great way to genuinely care for others is practicing daily for yourself.

There is nothing selfish about that.

It is smart.

Looking out for yourself is also strategic. If your line of work includes helping others on a daily basis, looking out for yourself can prevent you from becoming overwhelmed and distressed or becoming aloof, cold, and disconnected.

Ashley Womble helps us understand exactly what self-care is and what it is not:

The self-care I want to talk about is not getting a mani/pedi, haircut, or wax. That's not self-care. It's grooming. I believe that self-care is taking care of yourself with the goal of managing your stress and emotions.[119]

Womble goes on to list twenty easy, daily practices, including this: practice deep breathing, keep a journal, recite positive affirmations, make a gratitude list, and take a walk, ideally in nature. Again, there is nothing soft about this. It is about you taking care of yourself. It is smart.

As mentioned on day 11 ("reflection"), Dr. Kristin Neff reminds us to have self-compassion. She refers to looking after yourself, which includes not being too hard on yourself, especially when things don't go your way. She explains:

Self-compassion does not try to capture and define the worth or essence of who we are. It is not a thought or label, a judgement or an evaluation ... Rather than managing our self-image so that it is always palatable, self-compassion honors the fact that all human beings have both strengths and weaknesses.

... Self-compassion steps in precisely where self-esteem lets us down—whenever we fail or feel inadequate.[120]

If we get caught up in other people's crises and emotions (that's emotional contagion), we'll be in crisis too, we won't be able to help that person, and we'll be of no help to ourselves. Don't misread this, because—again—it is normal to feel hurt, sadness, and anger and to be bothered by the terrible situations some people are in.

It is self-control (and grit, and resilience, and calm, and ... you get the point—each of the previous keywords) and your perspective that allow you to be motivated to action *that is rationally based*. You are keeping your emotions in check (not ignoring them) while your breathing exercises and awareness practices help you handle those tough moments.

The other end of the extreme is becoming numb to the pain and suffering of others. That is definitely a coping strategy but one that is not positive or healthy (nor one that **warr;or21** endorses). Ignoring emotions (ours and those of others) as well as people's suffering might get you through that moment, but it will have long-term, negative consequences.

Dr. Helen Riess shares one easy way to control your emotions to help you avoid becoming overwhelmed with other people's issues, problems, and stressors:

It's important to recognize that labeling the emotion to the best of your ability is the first step in trying orient yourself to essential personal data without which you can't be fully present or attuned to the person with whom you are speaking.

If you're trying to encourage, inspire, soothe, or hold someone accountable for her actions, you first must try to understand which emotional platform you are starting from; otherwise there is little chance for effective communication.[121]

Dr. Alice Boyes adds more, especially when it is negative emotions:

Being able to accept and tolerate negative emotions opens up a world of possibility for what you can accomplish, allows you to choose the most meaningful path over the most comfortable one, and will help you reach your potential.

It is normal to feel certain emotions when engaging someone going through tough times. The key is again, not "catching" those

emotions and being overwhelmed and consumed with them.[122]

Boyes states it is not being afraid of those emotions, which are normal:

If you don't fear that uncomfortable emotions will overwhelm you, cause you to become out of control, or lead you to you
doing something out of character, you'll be
largely able to experience emotional discomfort without being distressed by it.[123]

When you are expressing sympathy, remember that you do not have to fix
or solve their issues. Being there for them, demonstrating empathy (day
13), and listening is incredibly powerful. Using these skills lets that person
know you genuinely care, and it will help give them clarity on what to do.

Crisis Text Line calls this *helping move the person from their "hot moment"
to a "cooler calm."* Note, this is the opposite of telling them what to do or
how to feel, judging, being critical, or minimizing their feelings. Instead,
the previously explained approach is the best, research-backed way to
most effectively help them—having sympathy and compassion while
your wisdom (day 9) is making sure you are helping them in a manner
that is beneficial.

Remember, it is about knowing the skills and then using those skills genuinely. Finally, continually helping others is tough work, and it is draining.
Don't forget to take care of yourself first and constantly.

Let's end today with useful information and research from the great people at Greater Good:

Compassion is not the same as empathy or altruism, though the concepts are related. While empathy refers more generally to our ability to take the perspective of and feel the emotions of another person, compassion is when those feelings and thoughts include the desire to help. Altruism, in turn, is the kind, selfless behavior often prompted by feelings of compassion, though one can feel compassion without acting on it, and altruism isn't always motivated by compassion.

While cynics may dismiss compassion as touchy-feely or irrational, scientists have started to map the biological basis of compassion, suggesting its deep evolutionary purpose. This research has shown that when we feel compassion, our heart rate slows down, we secrete the "bonding hormone" oxytocin, and regions of the brain linked to empathy, caregiving, and feelings of pleasure light up, which often results in our wanting to approach and care for other people.[124]

Reflection

Remember, demonstrating care for others is about perspective—their perspective. Ensure that what you are intending to do is being received the same way as you intend it when seeking to help others in their struggles. It is many of the little things that add up to show genuine care.

Also, take a moment before the end of the day to reflect on taking care of yourself. Check in with yourself like you did on day 11. Are you getting enough exercise? Are you sleeping enough? What about your eating habits? Finally, are you making sure to spend time with people who care about you, and are you surrounding yourself with other gritty people (day 4)?

Let today be a day where you make sure you show compassion—and start by showing it to yourself.

Onward!

Evening Practice

In your notebook, write down answers to the following questions, remembering not to repeat your previous responses:

1. One thing that made you happy today
2. One nice thing someone did for you today
3. One nice thing you did for someone today

Day 15: Awe

> Look for more daily experiences of awe. This doesn't
> require a trek to the mountains. What the sci-
> ence of awe suggests is that opportunities for awe
> surround us, and their benefits are profound.
> —Dacher Keltner

Morning Breathing Practice

- As early as possible after you wake up, dedicate five minutes to breathing to help you get focused for the day and realize that you are setting your perspective.
- Start off with four minutes of four-by-four breathing (four seconds inhaling and four seconds exhaling). Remember, you can use the animated shield graphic here if you need to: https://www.warrior21.com/breathe.
- Next, do the 4-7-8 breathing exercise.[125]

LET'S EXPLORE TODAY'S KEYWORD, AWE, to understand its impact on resilience and positive mental health. Having today's keyword be *awe* might come as a surprise to some. Why is awe important to a twenty-one-day practice on resilience and positive mental health?

Once again, it is all about perspective (by the way, this conveniently connects with tomorrow's keyword, which is no surprise—perspective!). Just as a gratitude practice each evening helps shape our perspective, reminding us that there are good things occurring in our life each day, finding something each day that has put you in awe can serve as a reminder that there are amazing things all around you.

Let's first explore what awe is, since it is so important to being more positive and contributes to our inner strength, positive mental health, and resilience. According to Dr. Jennifer Stellar, awe is the following (as explained in Sarah DiGiulo's article):

The emotion we feel in response to something vast that defies our existing frame of reference in one area or another, and leads us to change our perception of that frame of reference.[126]

Dr. Amie Gordon adds:

It's how we respond when we see something new or novel that doesn't fit with our understanding of the world.[127]

And for good measure, here's one more doctor, Michelle Shiota, offering her version:

These experiences can make people feel awe, or an overwhelming feeling of wonder.[128]

These explanations remind us of how closely awe is connected to our perspective. By the way and for clarity, Gordon is referring to something not fitting with our understanding of the world as a good thing.

This reminds me of curiosity. Awe is not the same as simply sensing the beauty of something either. That's something different. Here's something else about awe: it makes us feel small, in a good way. Sarah DiGiulo again explains what Gordon means:

One important distinction between awe and other emotions (like inspiration or surprise) is that awe makes us feel small — or feel a sense of "self-diminishment" in science-speak. And that's good for us.

We spend a lot of our time thinking about what's going on in our world and what's affecting us directly. Awe changes that, making us see ourselves as a small piece of something larger.

Feeling small makes us feel humbled (thereby lessening selfish tendencies like entitlement, arrogance, and narcissism). And feeling small and humbled makes us want to engage with others and feel more connected to others.

All of that is important for wellbeing.[129]

The science shows the benefits of being in awe.[130] We feel small in a good way, it humbles us, it increases our desire to connect with others, and it can increase our immune health.

Another research study[131] has connected the following with being in awe: enhanced critical and creative thinking, improved health, and an increase in prosocial behaviors such as kindness, self-sacrifice, cooperation and resource sharing. Hopefully now you're starting to see that being in awe is not a childish concept. Awe is a genuinely important concept that needs to be practiced.

This article detailing Dr. Michelle Liota's work offers some examples and provides more on the benefits that awe can provide:

People can experience awe when confronted with a vast natural landscape, like Zion or the Grand Canyon, or when listening to extraordinary, complex music. People might also feel awe when witnessing an extraordinary act by another person or while viewing art that changes how they see the world.

The emotion of awe is likely specific to humans, but is not specific to one culture. Across the world, different cultures create and honor awe-evoking places like Notre Dame in Paris or the ancient pyramids of Egypt.

When people feel awe, their mind clears and their attention becomes focused on the extraordinary thing evoking this emotion. These effects can be thought of as a temporary form of mindfulness. Usually mindfulness requires extensive training and effort, but Shiota suggested that awe-induced mindfulness happens automatically.[132]

Awe is not limited to visiting the wonders of the world (thankfully, as your budget most likely will not allow you to visit each!). Sure, visiting the Grand Canyon can surely elicit awe, but so too can our daily experiences. Christopher Bergland offers his experiences of awe:

When the daffodils bloom, I'm reminded that peak experiences and a sense of awe can literally be found in your backyard.

As a kid, I was awestruck by the scope of towering skyscrapers as I walked around the streets of Manhattan. Skyscrapers made me feel small but the sea of humanity on the city streets made me feel connected to a collective that was much bigger than myself.[133]

Awe-inspiring things are everywhere around us. With our practice of pausing (day 6) already well established, we can now add awe to it as well. By the way, let's pause for a moment (ahh, yes, pun definitely intended!). You well might already do this. That's great and *awe*some (okay, no more puns, I promise).

Don't forget that part of this **warr;or21** journey is helping you acknowledge the practices you were already doing before this program. It very well could be you are now learning the terms behind your practices and research-backed reasons why they are so effective. This is how personal growth and inner strength is enhanced. You've moved past just doing things here and there. You now know what works, why it works, and how the practices are connected.

Now, back to awe and how it is also connected to one of the pillars of resilience—purpose. Awe helps you see beyond your individual goals and intensifies your purpose to help others. Dr. Paul Piff and his team explored awe in a research study and shared the following:

Across all these different elicitors of awe, we found the same sorts of effects—people felt smaller, less self-important, and behaved in a more prosocial fashion.

Might awe cause people to become more invested in the greater good, giving more to charity, volunteering to help others, or doing more to lessen their impact on the environment? Our research would suggest that the answer is yes.[134]

Again, let's not lose the perception you have been building. We must not forget that the primary focus of **warr;or21** is the inward journey of resilience and mental health. That said, awe reminds us that the outward journey occurs at the same time.

Dacher Keltner emphasizes the benefits of awe for the individual and others:

Take the time to pause and open your mind to those things which you do not fully understand. You will be the better for it—and, as your feelings of awe ripple out through acts of kindness, so will the rest of us.[135]

This outward journey in each of our worlds contains elements of awe everywhere if we pause to look for it and allow ourselves to experience it. The result, after feeling awe—which is a reward itself—is increasing your capacity to help others.

Reflection

If you live in a big city, consider looking up at the beautiful architecture. In a small town? Stop to reflect on a design of a building you see every day. If you're in a rural area, notice something small, like an individual flower or branch, and then look at the larger landscape. Appreciate it and realize how it is part of something grander.

Today, make sure you look at things differently. See the small things that you might not have been pausing to stop and acknowledge. But it is more than that. Find yourself in awe.

Take some time today to watch the awe-inspiring video below. After watching it, reflect on how it is closely connected to the guided imagery practice you have already done and how it impacts your senses—sights, touch, smells, sounds, and taste.

Throughout the day and for the remaining days, find at least one thing that puts you in awe. This will now be part of your daily gratitude practice each evening.

Awe video: https://ggia.berkeley.edu/practice/awe_video.

Evening Practice

In your notebook, write down answers to the following questions, remembering not to repeat your previous responses:

1. One thing that made you happy today
2. One nice thing someone did for you today
3. One nice thing you did for someone today
4. One thing that put you in awe today

Bonus: #RealConvo

Healing takes time, and asking for
help is a courageous step.
—Mariska Hargitay

THIS IS A NOT A day that is part of the **warr;or21** program, but it is extremely important.

It is a call to action.

It is a reminder.

Take a moment to pause.

Check in with yourself and genuinely see how you are doing. Yes, **warr;or21** is about building resilience, further developing your inner strength, and enhancing your positive mental health. Recall the disclaimer in the beginning; if you need the help of a therapist or doctor, this program is not designed to replace that.

As previously shared, resilience also means getting help from others if you need it. Much like how someone goes to the doctor for a broken limb, if you are having issues with a mental health condition, such as depression or anxiety, or you're not sure what it is but you know something seems not right, seek professional help.

You don't have to take it on by yourself. You have shown and proven to yourself that you have strength by sticking with **war;or21**. Don't forget that real strength also means realizing you don't have to take everything on by yourself. People care about you, and help is available. Resilience is also letting others help you.

If you are doing well, that is great news. I mean it, yet it does not end there.

Check in with someone you know who is having a hard time. Odds are you know someone going through a relationship issue, a bad breakup, work concerns, financial worries, or some other personal stressor.

Let them know that they are not alone. You don't have to fix their issues or problems; that's not your job or responsibility. Be there to listen and let them know that you genuinely care.

That is the essence of #RealConvo (created by my great friends at AFSP[136]); check in with someone and have a real conversation. It will make a difference—a big difference. Trust me.

Law enforcement officers, check out "Law Enforcement Suicide: How Police and First-Responders Can Support One Another's Mental Health."[137]

For everyone (including law enforcement officers), check out how to start a #RealConvo in "Crisis Negotiation: How to Talk to Someone You're Worried About"[138] and "How to Start (and Continue!) a Conversation About Mental Health: A #RealConvo Guide from AFSP."[139]

Finally, learn more by visiting the National Alliance on Mental Illness[140] and the American Association of Suicidology.[141]

Day 16: Perspective

> When you can't control what's happening, challenge yourself to control how you respond to what's happening. That's where your power is.
>
> —Unknown

Morning Breathing Practice

- As early as possible after you wake up, dedicate five minutes to breathing to help you get focused for the day and realize that you are setting your perspective. Enjoy it. Do it because you want to do it. Wire your brain this morning to show you are taking control and choosing to do this.
- Start off with two minutes of breathing. Just concentrate on your in and out breaths while breathing naturally.
- Next, do two minutes of guided breathing. As you breathe in, say to yourself, "I am strong." As you breathe out, say to yourself, "I am calm."
- Lastly, do the 4-7-8 breathing exercise.[142]

PERSPECTIVE, TODAY'S KEYWORD, REMINDS US that although we can experience the same incident or situation as others, we might all experience it differently. Our perceptions can vary, and each person involved in the same situation can have different perspectives, emotions, and actions. When we fail to take this into account, how often do we apologetically say, "Sorry, I didn't realize you saw it differently from how I do"?

When we pause, it allows us to stop and see how others might be interpreting things differently from the way we are. This is the essence of developing empathy. It helps us understand other people's perspectives and then helps us respond and act in the most appropriate manner.

Pausing also helps us catch ourselves, preventing us from making snap judgments about people. Otherwise, taking a negative approach could lead us to becoming cynical, telling others how they should feel, minimizing their emotions, and minimizing their perspective when it differs from our own.

Our perspective can either help us increase our grit and resilience or it can diminish our feelings of self-worth, pushing us toward a downward cycle of negative thoughts and feelings.

Being able to recall past, positive events helps the brain rewire from focusing on the negative toward remembering (and reflecting on) good things that have happened. Dr. Alex Korb explains:

Remembering positive events has a two-fold effect: it directly increases serotonin and indirectly keeps you from remembering negative events.[143]

Managing our thoughts, emotions, and actions can help us persevere. In tough moments, it helps us handle ourselves and make decisions that are not emotionally driven but instead grounded in a controlling manner that is rationally based. This is what the **warr;or** way is all about.

Dr Kelli Harding states:

The more a person labels a situation as harmful or stressful, the more toxic it becomes.[144]

Harding continues by adding how important perspective is during tough
moments:

Our ability to reframe adversity in a positive
light is an important component of stress
relief.[145]

In those moments that are negative for us, we can still learn. As we
pause for a moment, this is arguably the toughest part to grasp on the
warr;or21 journey. We can't control everything, and yes, failure will
occur and negative things will happen throughout our lives in varying
degrees. Like grit (day 4), ultimately it is about perspective and what
we do next.

As Dr. Harding explained above, it is about perspective and, more specifically, reframing. Dr. Rick Hanson further explains:

In particular, finding positive meaning in
negative events, which is called reframing,
is helpful for coping and recovery. This is not
to suggest that a tough experience is any
less painful, or that it is alright for people to
mistreat you. My point is that even a horrible
event or situation may have some opportunities in it for a positive experience.[146]

Now perhaps you were like me when first reading the above and began thinking of actual or potential worst-case scenarios that discount or negate the possibility of reframing. Well, Hanson talks about his personal battle with cancer, while other stories he shares are about Holocaust survivors, the tragic events of the 9/11 terrorist attacks, and soldiers who survived being held prisoner in atrocious conditions. Like I said, this is heavy stuff and arguably the toughest to grasp.

It is all about today's keyword—perspective—and you are further developing it. You just read about Hanson's perspective, and Reivich and Shatté now further elaborate and share their perspective to help you develop yours:

In some cases, events are so severe that your reactions are driven by the event itself, not your beliefs about the event. When a loved one dies, the emotions that follow largely stem from the tragedy itself, not from one's interpretations of the tragedy.

In the hours or days after a disaster—such as September 11—the magnitude of the event dictates your beliefs, and questioning their accuracy or usefulness is not particularly useful.[147]

Both Reivich and Shatté add the following just after the above passage:

This fact does not mean that one's beliefs play no role in healing from tragedies and that the ABC skill[148] serves no purpose. To

the contrary, your beliefs and resilience determine how quickly and how easily you will
regain control of your emotions and behaviors following colossal experiences.[149]

That's a lot to take in, and perhaps the above snippets are worth reading again.

Don't forget, I said part of **warr;or21** was pushing you out of your comfort zone. Admittedly, reframing is something I still grapple with. Perhaps this moment can serve as a reminder that although you are on an individual journey, resilience means if you have experienced something horrible in your life or have trouble coping sometimes, you don't have to take it on alone. True resilience means reaching out for help, and that too is brave. When I say, "This is the way," it does not mean you have to venture alone. Help is available, and that too is being a **warr;or**.

Another critical aspect to resilience is our perspective on optimism. Our positive perspective and outlook is necessary to have resilience and positive mental health. Southwick and Charney describe this as being positive reappraisal:

Positive reappraisal requires us to find alternative positive meaning for neutral or negative events, situations, and/or beliefs. While
this remarkable woman suffered profoundly,
from her Holocaust experiences [they were
referring to a woman who survived the
Holocaust and was having nightmares years
later], she somehow found a way to reappraise her nightmares.

Although she was unable to control the nightmares, she was able to view them as powerful reminders that she was lucky to have survived and now had the privilege of waking up each morning to a new day.[150]

Southwick and Cherney further add that the process of positive reappraisal is directly connected to resilience:

Numerous researchers have found that the capacity to positively reframe and extract meaning from adversity is an important component of stress resilience: resilient individuals often find that trauma has forced them to learn something new or to grow as a person.[151]

They go on to list many benefits of positive reappraisal, and doing this corresponds with the four pillars of resilience as part of the **warr;or21** program: awareness, health, purpose, and positivity.

Having a positive perspective can also be applied with forward thinking. Our positive perspective in regard to forward thinking must not be foolish and must be an unachievable type of optimism. It has to be realistic. Reivich and Shatté explain this as being "realistic optimism":

The ability to maintain a positive outlook without denying reality, actively appreciating the positive aspects of a situation without ignoring the negative aspects. It means aspiring and hoping for positive outcomes, and working toward those outcomes, without assuming that those outcomes are a forgone conclusion.[152]

So, our positive perspective must also be realistic while we remain optimistic and hopeful. We do not ignore our emotions or negative elements of the situation; instead, we do the best we can, and regardless of the outcome, we learn from it.

Southwick and Charney explain:

As do pessimists, realistic optimists pay close attention to negative information that is relevant to the problem they face. However, unlike pessimists, they do not remain focused on the negative.[153]

To conclude, here are practical ways to build realistic optimism. Southwick and Charney add the following:

1. Focus attention on the positive things around us.
2. Intentionally think positive thoughts and do not dwell on negative thoughts.
3. Reframe the negative and interpret events in a more positive light.
4. Behave and take action in ways that build positive feelings.[154]

Perspective is about gaining wisdom from the past and understanding what we are experiencing in this very moment. It can help us go forward.

It all depends if we view it a certain way.

As you read today, this is critical in those moments that are not easy and involve hurt and suffering. Our perspective cannot change the past, but it can help us handle it now and not let it dictate who we are today and who we are going forward.

Onward, **warr;or**. You got this.

Reflection

Today's reflection comes from Dr. Rick Hanson:

In recent events in your past, look for times when you were strong. Perhaps you called on your body to keep standing during a long day at work or to continue running during a workout.

Perhaps you stuck up for yourself or for someone else. Maybe you got something done even though you wanted to quit. Let the ideas of these times become a felt sense of strength.[155]

You are strong, and you always were. Today, take the time to reflect it on it.

Evening Practice

In your notebook, write down answers to the following questions, remembering not to repeat your previous responses:

1. One thing that made you happy today
2. One nice thing someone did for you today
3. One nice thing you did for someone today
4. One thing that put you in awe today

Don't forget about today's keyword, perspective, and how important it is when creating new habits. Here, as you start the last full week of **warr;or21**, think about how you are rewiring your brain. That truly is control. Your breath is your anchor, and your perspective helps you navigate going forward.

Make sure you are not just going through the motion or, worse, feeling like it is a chore. Enjoy the journey. After all, there is awe, and positive things are all around. We just have to pause and reflect on it. Onward, **warr;or.**

Day 17: Smile

> Success is no accident. It is hard work, persever-
> ance, learning, studying, sacrifice, and most of
> all, love of what you are doing or learning.
> —Pele

Morning Breathing Practice

* As early as possible after you wake up, dedicate five minutes to breathing to help you get focused for the day and realize that you are setting your perspective.
* Start off with two minutes of four-by-six breathing. Instead of exhaling for four seconds, now try to do it for six seconds.
* Next, do two minutes of guided breathing. As you breathe in, smile and say to yourself, "I am smiling." As you breathe out, release the smile and say to yourself, "I am ready." Ready for what? Your day of course!
* Next, do the 4-7-8 breathing exercise for the last minute.[156]

SMILING IS SERIOUS BUSINESS THESE Days, and numerous studies have been conducted on what seems to be a simple act. The truth is simply smiling has big implications, and the research backs that claim.

Before we continue, as you read this, do yourself a favor. Smile. Smile and say in your head the following: "You have some great dedication. You are taking care of yourself, and you should be proud."

Again, this is not soft. This is a hardcore strategy.

How so?

Words of self-encouragement are not often written to say, "*I* should be proud," but instead say "*you*." Why? Because research shows[157] that self-encouragement is important, and so is specifically how you do it (using "you" instead of "I").

Susan York Morris explains:

The report goes on to say that using the third person in self-talk can help you step back and think more objectively about your response and emotions, whether you're thinking about a past event or looking into the future. It can also help you reduce stress and anxiety.[158]

It can also help counter negative, self-deprecating statements and ruminating. It might feel a bit odd or awkward at first, but think about how that was most likely the case with many other **warr;or21** practices you started more than sixteen days ago. You've pushed yourself out of your comfort zone, and you have shown it is for the better. Do it again by trying this out.

If you're interested in the science behind why smiling is so beneficial, you can read more about why "You Should Smile Every Day."[159] Below is a quick snapshot:

- Smiling makes you more attractive.
- Smiling relieves stress.
- Smiling elevates your mood.
- Smiling is contagious.
- Smiling boosts your immune system.
- Smiling lowers your blood pressure.
- Smiling makes you feel good.
- Smiling helps you stay positive.

When you think about the seriousness of the work you do every day and the daily stressful encounters you face, smiling (of course at the appropriate times), just like your evening gratitude practices, reminds you of the goodness you deserve to feel.

What about if you feel like you're stuck in a bad mood? Smiling, even if you don't feel like it, can help change your perspective and bring you happiness. Really.

Nicole Spector shares the research on this:

Ever had someone tell you to cheer up and smile? It's probably not the most welcomed advice, especially when you're feeling sick, tired or just plain down in the dumps.

But there's actually good reason to turn that frown upside down, corny as it sounds. Science has shown that the mere act of smiling can lift your mood, lower stress, boost your immune system and possibly even prolong your life.[160]

One more tip for escaping your bad mood and thoughts and turning toward happiness and grit (plus adding a smile to it) comes from Maria Brilaki:

If you could just add a harmless "but" to every negative thought you produced, you could transform all negative thoughts into positive ones …

[two examples]:

- "I feel like I will never lose weight" becomes "I feel like I will never lose weight, but I know there are other people who used to be exactly like me and made it happen!"
- "I will never find love" becomes "I will never find love if I keep staying at home just like I am right now. But if I start going out more, my luck might change."[161]

Also, note how today's quote does not mention the keyword. After reading the quote, however, it is hard not to smile when thinking about how it applies to your successes in life. Think about at least three things that have made you successful.

They did not come easily, but doesn't it feel good now? Also, think about your service to others and helping them in their successes. That, too, is the source of your smile.

Dr. Jeremy Dean shares some easy, practical tips that can increase our happiness and lead to more smiling in our daily lives:

What's the number one strategy that people use to feel better, increase their energy levels and reduce tension? Exercise.

It doesn't have to be a marathon; a simple walk around the block will do the trick. We all know it'll make us feel better to get out and stretch our legs, but there are always excuses to avoid it.

… Number two on the list of all-time top strategies people use for feeling better is: listening to music.

Music can influence mood in many ways but most people rate its power to manage our positive moods as the top reason they love music. We particularly like the fact that it can make our good moods even better.[162]

On day 4, we learned that a key aspect to having grit is surrounding yourself with gritty people. The benefits of spending time with like-minded people can be applied here as well. Being around happy people makes it easier to smile, and it's backed by science. Dr. Kelli Harding shares:

Positive relationships lower stress, cortisol, inflammation, pain and blood pressure.

They boost immune functioning, mood and recovery after injury. Supportive relationships can also help people with serious disease and cancer live longer.[163]

Much like awe (day 15) is about seeing and appreciating the little things, the impact of smiling is similar.

Dr. Rick Hanson explains more:

> Enjoying the taste of toasted raisin bread or the humor in a cartoon may not seem like much, but simple pleasures like these ease emotional upsets, lift your mood, and enrich your life. They also provide health benefits, by releasing endorphins and natural opioids that shift you out of stressful, draining reactive states and into happier responsive ones.
>
> ... Opportunities for pleasure are all around you, especially if you include things like the rainbow glitter of the tiny grains of sand in a sidewalk, the sound of water falling into a tub, the sense of connection in talking with a friend, or the reassurance that comes that comes from the stove working when you need to make dinner.[164]

It's the little things that add up that are meaningful. The question is, Are you letting those smiling moments occur?

Reflection

Today, try to smile a bit more than usual. Say hello to a few extra people and share a smile while doing it. When someone does something nice for you (like opening a door or holding it for you), say thank you and give them a smile.

Finally, reflect again on your **warr;or21** journey. Hopefully here at day 17 you are enjoying it. It is not supposed to be easy all the time, and it does not remove the hard things in life. The purpose is to help you handle things and persevere. Make sure to take time today to smile to yourself about what you have accomplished. For example, check out your notebook and look at the things you have written the past sixteen days. Onward because this is the **warr;or** way.

Evening Practice

In your notebook, write down answers to the following questions, remembering not to repeat your previous responses:

1. One thing that made you happy today
2. One nice thing someone did for you today
3. One nice thing you did for someone today
4. One thing that put you in awe today

Day 18: Adapt

Patience is the calm acceptance that things can happen
in a different order than the one you have in mind.
—David G. Allen

Morning Breathing Practice

- As early as possible after you wake up, dedicate five minutes to breathing to help you get focused for the day and realize that you are setting your perspective.
- Start off with four minutes of 4four-by-six breathing. Instead of exhaling for four seconds, now try to do it for six seconds.
- Next, do the 4-7-8 breathing exercise. It's all about control. Don't forget it starts with your breathing.[165]

ON THE SURFACE, TODAY'S KEYWORD, adapt, can create confusion, as it can be perceived as contradictory to previously discussed important terms like grit (day 4) and resilience (day 8). With grit and resilience, we learned to never give up but instead to push forward and persevere. One could then view adapting as giving in and giving up.

Nope, that's not what adapting is at all.

Adapting means embracing the concepts of grit and resilience while not disregarding other key terms, such as practice (day 7), reflection (day 11), and, importantly, wisdom (day 9). To put it as a simple math formula, here's one way to see the resilient formula of *adapt*:

Knowledge + Skills = Adapt

The above formula can serve as a reminder that through our experiences and practicing with intent,[166] we learn the necessary skills to be successful in life and enhance our mental health. This wisdom, along with life experiences, teaches us valuable lessons. Not everything will go as planned, and struggles we did not foresee will present themselves. It is in those moments that, when properly assessed, our knowledge and skills will allow us to adapt.

Life is not a cookie-cut design, and your approach, even in well-planned moments, will not always go to plan, despite your best efforts. Instead of mindlessly doing the same thing over and over again, at times you must adapt your approach. Stopping to pause and reflect allows you to realize that sometimes your current approach just isn't working.

The nonresilient person might quit, and the foolish person will keep making the same mistakes, but you, the **warr;or**, knows better. You learn, you adapt, and you figure out a new way by changing your perspective (day 16) and seeing things a different way. The **warr;or** in you has developed a way to reappraise the situation. You see it differently. In those instances where you did not succeed, you learn to "fail better"[167] and rebound from setbacks.[168] Your perspective and reappraisal allow you to adjust and make new, better decisions.

Things don't always go as planned. Adapting is critical. Dr. Leah Weiss shares:

"Good in the beginning, good in the middle, good in the end" doesn't mean that everything always unfolds according to plan. It doesn't mean we always get what we want.[169]

Being able to adapt and reflect, according to Weiss, allows us to continually get better:

We can see the events more clearly and respond more skillfully.[170]

Pointedly, Martin Seligman describes adapting as a key function of resilience, as it has to do with not giving up:

People who don't give up have a habit of interpreting setbacks as temporary, local, and changeable.[171]

Mitchell Lee Marks, Philip Mirvis, and Ron Ashkenas explain how you can adapt when things do not go as planned. This includes the tip below, which involves honest reflecting on what went wrong and what role you had in contributing to it:

Figure Out Why You Lost: … as social psychologists have found in decades' worth of studies, high achievers usually take too much credit for their successes and assign too much external blame for their failures. It's a type of attribution bias that protects self-esteem but also prevents learning and growth. People focus on situational factors or company politics instead of examining their own role in the problem.

... Those who rebound from career losses take a decidedly different approach. Instead of getting stuck in grief or blame, they actively explore how they contributed to what went wrong, evaluate whether they sized up the situation correctly and reacted appropriately, and consider what they would do differently if given the chance.

They also gather feedback from a wide variety of people (including superiors, peers, and subordinates), making it clear that they want honest feedback, not consolation.[172]

Looking back on previous keywords and reflecting on their impact with the ability to adapt helps you see how interconnected each day of the **warr;or21** program is and how they builds off of one another. Wisdom, practice, grit, calm, and reflection build your inner strength so you can avoid being fixed in your ways and allow for change. Gilkey and Kilts describe this as cognitive fitness:

The more cognitively fit you are, the better you will be able to make decisions, solve problems, and deal with stress and change.

Cognitive fitness will allow you to be more open to new ideas and alternative perspectives. It will give you the capacity to change your behaviors and forecast their outcomes in order to realize your goals.[173]

According to Dr. Alex Korb, making decisions, such as adapting, helps reduce anxiety and worrying.[174] This type of taking control over what we can moves beyond perception; it becomes our reality. Making the decision to adapt is healthy in tough situations. You are able to focus on how to succeed instead of getting stuck on the negative. This version of being stuck can lead to ruminating and falling into the downward cycle of getting overwhelmed with emotions like stress and fear.

Adapting does not guarantee automatic success, but life experiences tell you that it increases your chances.

Still trying to grasp the concept of sticking with the same process versus adapting? A wise person shared great advice with me when I was in a tough situation. In that situation, I felt like I was being mistreated, cheated, and not respected in my workplace. His sage advice I continue to reflect on to this day. The following statement helped me then and continues to today when I am conflicted with sticking it out or realizing I need to adapt because it's not working—or, even worse, I'm only making things worse. The wise words are these: when you find yourself in a hole, stop digging.

For me, the negative aspects weren't ignored, but I started to look at them for their relevance. I told myself to fix what I could and move on where I couldn't—and always learn from it. This type of practice, like the other **warr;or21** practices, increases your wisdom and makes you stronger. It also helps with developing positive mental health.

Here is another example of this approach to help you adjust and practice empathy on yourself.

Change the perspective.

Imagine if instead of it being you going through the situation, it was someone close to you who you care about. What advice would you share with that person to help them get through things?

Jeff Thompson, Ph.D.

Dr. Stephen Sideroff follows this up with then asking yourself the following questions:

> Would you make such harsh judgements about them? Would you dismiss or minimize their achievements the way you do with your own? When you recognize that you would treat this other person differently than you are treating yourself, it supports your efforts to label as inappropriate, your old beliefs.[175]

The ability to adapt is a strong habit to have, and you build it by actually doing it (adapting). An easy first step to building this type of realistic optimism is simply envisioning a positive outcome.[176] Research shows that thinking positive thoughts builds a positive mind-set.[177]

Your continued practice, including breathing, helps you maintain focus. Through your breathing, your focus and ability to stay calm can help you think more clearly and better manage your emotions.[178]

This should remind you of day 2 and the triangle's first element—your thinking. Through your purposeful thinking (and reflecting), you are able to try different skills, and you are also able to use the same skills differently. By doing so, you are putting various keywords into actual practice. The ability to adapt is a true sign of resilience, wisdom, and looking out for your mental health.

Adapting and decision-making are also about control. Korb explains:

> The important thing here is not actual control but perceived control. Making decisions may not increase your actual control over a

situation, but it will likely increase your perceived control. And when you increase your
perceived control, you increase your confidence, mood, and future decision-making
capabilities.[179]

As you enter day 18, you are now realizing how closely the keywords are
linked. As you reflect on today's quote, your ability to adapt is a true rep-
resentation of understanding what you can control and what you can't.
You never give up, yet you also use your knowledge to know when to
reappraise and adjust.

Reflection

Take some time today to reflect on how grit, resilience, and perseverance
are being complemented by your ability to adapt. Remember, the first
three words are not supposed to make you stubborn. When wisdom is
applied, instead of being stubborn, it gives you the knowledge to adapt.

Evening Practice

In your notebook, write down answers to the following questions, remembering not to repeat your previous responses:

1. One thing that made you happy today
2. One nice thing someone did for you today
3. One nice thing you did for someone today
4. One thing that put you in awe today

Day 19: Mindfulness

There's a stereotype this makes you soft. No,
[mindfulness] makes you on point.
—Major General Walter Piatt, US Army

Morning Breathing Practice

- As early as possible after you wake up, dedicate five minutes to breathing to help you get focused for the day and realize that you are setting your perspective.
- Start off with one minute of four-by-six breathing. Instead of exhaling for four seconds, now try to do it for six seconds.
- Next, do the 4-7-8 breathing exercise.[180]
- Now let's do guided imagery with our breathing. Think of a favorite place you enjoy going to. Shortly, you will close your eyes, picturing it. As you do, experience it with your senses.

  o What are four things you see?
  o What are three different things you can touch? What does each feel like?
  o What are two different things you can hear?
  o What is one thing you can smell?
  o Finally, describe how you feel while experiencing this.

MINDFULNESS IS A TERM THAT connotes many different things in many different people. For law enforcement officers (among many other professions), it could have some negative connotations.

Dr. Stephanie Conn shares more on this potential perspective of mindfulness in her book on law enforcement resilience:

Most people think of mindfulness as some kind of spiritual voodoo for hipsters. On the contrary, it's about practicing non-judgment of the self, giving yourself and others compassion. It's about being open, curious, and present to the moment instead of fighting with it.[181]

Those are some powerful words to reflect on. The present moment is here no matter what. The question is, How are you approaching it and what is your perspective? Are you embracing it or seeing it as something to fight with? Having mindfulness allows you to accept the present moment. Next, it allows you to figure out what to do next while pausing.

A group you might not expect to practice mindfulness is the military. Here's some research on how it is helping them, according to the *NY Times*:

The paper, in the journal Progress in Brain Research, reported that the troops who went through a monthlong training regimen that included daily practice in mindful breathing and focus techniques were better able to discern key information under chaotic circumstances and experienced increases in working memory function. The soldiers also reported making fewer cognitive errors than service members who did not use mindfulness.[182]

If mindfulness can help with the tense and stressful moments soldiers face, surely it can be applied elsewhere.

Back to Dr. Conn, she explains how there is no finish line to mindfulness. Because mindfulness is being present in the moment, it is always a work in practice:

It's called "practice" because it requires continuous efforts to do it. It's a way of life, not tasks to be completed and things just become better.[183]

The above passage can be viewed as describing the **warr;or21** journey you are on. It's a continuous effort, yet it is not a task. You have been working on rewiring your brain as you become a better and internally stronger you. There are no shortcuts. It takes effort, and you have been putting it in—for nineteen days!

Pause for a moment and reflect on if the term *mindfulness* had been the keyword for one of the first days of this program. Compare how you might have felt then with how you feel about it now. Some people prefer using the term *awareness*, and others freely interchange the two.

Ask yourself if there is a difference between mindfulness and awareness.

The **warr;or21** program views the two as being similar; however, there is a much deeper meaning to mindfulness. It incorporates awareness but entails much more. Mindfulness is being fully aware in the present moment, which involves a purpose connected with nearly every other keyword in this program.

Think about it. That's intense. Empathy, adapting, calm, wisdom, breathing, grit and more are all involved in mindfulness.

Mindfulness is when it all comes together in a way, without negative stress. It is a sense of being in the moment and being ready. Remember, **warr;or21** is a practice that is about taking care of yourself by building resilience and further enhancing your mental health.

Mindfulness involves acknowledging your current emotions and not ignoring them. This helps you maintain control of yourself and allows you to manage your emotions to ensure they do not dictate your actions (and then thinking) in a negative way. Mindfulness also helps you collect your thoughts to stop and become aware of what you are thinking.

It is worth reexamining what was previously shared by Dr. Leah Weiss with respect to emotions. Now that you are exploring mindfulness, you are able to look deeper at the connection between mindfulness and emotions:

Being mindful of your emotions doesn't mean not having emotions ... a major function of mindfulness is to help you see the emotions for what they are: feedback on the world—no more, no less.[184]

Mindfulness allows you to understand the impact of emotions and their role in situations. Weiss shares:

It is important to keep in mind that while our emotions happen in response to situations,

situations don't create our emotional response. It is the way we interpret or appraise
a situation that creates our emotional response to it.[185]

And here, Weiss get straight to the point on the connection to mindfulness:

Mindfulness lets us "do" emotions differently. With mindfulness, we can, for example, recognize the emotion of anger before
it's too late and we've done or said something regrettable. Mindfulness gives us a
pause between feeling and action.[186]

For good measure and for me to really drive home the point of what
mindfulness is able to help with, Southwick and Charney state:

The practitioner of mindfulness learns to
develop calm and accepting awareness of
thoughts, emotions, perceptions, bodily sensations, and functions such as breathing.[187]

Southwick and Charney then add that the benefits of mindfulness can
include the following:

Through this practice, we can learn to tolerate negative emotions better without impul-
sively acting on them.[188]

Dr. Seth Gillihan explains some additional benefits of mindfulness:

- Greater awareness of our thoughts and emotions
- Better control of emotions
- Decreased reactivity[189]

Jill Suttie discussed the benefits of having a consistent (daily) mindfulness practice with respect to coping:

A great deal of research suggests that mind-fulness can help healthy people reduce their stress. And thanks to Jon-Kabat Zinn's pio-neering MBSR program, there's now a large body of research showing that mindfulness can help people cope with the pain, anxiety, depression, and stress that might accom-pany illness, especially chronic conditions.[190]

To put mindfulness into perspective, let's talk about how it feels. Hopefully, for you, it is that sensation while you are doing your breathing exercises and then even more so those sensations right after you finish. There are numerous ways to practice mindfulness (such as breathing practices, being in awe, and observing what is around you and the impact on each of your senses without judgment).

With today's reading material, you can realize that mindfulness is beyond your *thinking*. It impacts your feelings and your behavior. Mindfulness involves your presence at the cognitive, emotional, and physical levels, and when you are practicing it, you deepen your understanding of your purpose—a purpose that is looking out for your own well-being first and then helping others.

Reflection

Mindfulness is a word frequently discussed in the media, on the internet, and elsewhere. Take some time today to reflect on what it means with respect to the **warr;or21** program and to you. Have a conversation with someone you know to share with them your take on mindfulness and get their perspective as well.

Evening Practice

In your notebook, write down answers to the following questions, remembering not to repeat your previous responses:

1. One thing that made you happy today
2. One nice thing someone did for you today
3. One nice thing you did for someone today
4. One thing that put you in awe today

Day 20: Silence

Silence is a source of great strength.
—Lao Tzu

Morning Breathing Practice

- As early as possible after you wake up, dedicate five minutes to breathing to help you get focused for the day and realize that you are setting your perspective.
- Start off with four minutes of breathing. Just concentrate on your in and out breaths while breathing naturally.
- Next, do the 4-7-8 breathing exercise.[191]

SILENCE IS NOT SIMPLY THE absence of talking or any other sounds. Silence, when used properly as part of your **warr;or21** practice, is something much more than that. Silence allows you to pause and focus on your breathing, enhance your perspective, deepen your empathy and sympathy, manage your emotions, and reflect on gratitude. If you don't start with silence, it is easy to lose your concentration and become distracted.

Silence can be enjoyable too. Think about how silence can occur when you are comfortable being around someone. When you are close with that person, the silence can be a sign of contentment, being relaxed and at ease. Picture being with that person. It is something more than what can be described in words; it's a feeling.

This sensation is the opposite of awkward silence, where people incessantly try to continue talking to prevent even a few seconds of silence, which can feel like an eternity to them. For some, the awkwardness of silence starts at four seconds. You can check out more[192] on how awkward silence can cause stress, anxiety, and more.

Silence, when experiencing it alone, can bring a sense of joy, calm, and contentment. Picture a moment by yourself at the beach, watching a sunrise or sunset, or going for a walk by yourself. Even if that walk is in a bustling town or city, with noise all around you, your silence allows you to enjoy the moment in complete mindfulness (day 19).

The opposite of silence—noise—can be harmful. Did you know that exposure to prolonged or excessive noise[193] has been shown to cause a range of health problems to the point where the World Health Organization released a report in 2011 titled "Burden of Disease from Environmental Noise"[194]?

People new to embracing silence through mindfulness and breathing practices can complain about the inner churn or constant thoughts arising in their mind. Leah Weiss explains this as people thinking "that their self-awareness practice created this churn," when in reality it was always there.[195] Engaging in these practices of silence helps acknowledge the churn and then work past it.

What does science tell us about the benefits of silence? One study showed taking time out even just once a day provides benefits and helps reduce stress. Other advantages one can experience from the "hidden benefits"[196] of silence include the following:

- boosting the immune system
- lowering of blood pressure
- decreases cortisol and adrenaline levels (i.e., keeps you calm)
- helps regulate hormones
- provides relief for suffering from insomnia
- increases awareness
- heightens listening skills

Silence can be viewed as a type of mental sit-up; it strengthens the brain. Even just two minutes of silence has shown to relieve tension. In one particular study,[197] it was even more effective than listening to soothing music. Another study[198] showed that adding a nature walk to your practice of silence helps with enhancing your memory. Professor Jonathan Schooler[199] of UCAL said that sitting in silence and daydreaming has shown to help with being more creative. Psychologist Kelly McGonigal[200] adds that silence can help the mind be more creative.

An entire country supports silence. Finland emphasizes the value of silence so much that in 2011, they ran a tourism campaign promoting the slogan, "Silence, Please."[201]

Reivich and Shatté explain how two terms previously discussed during the **warr;or21** program, calm and focus, help during practices that include being silent. They describe them both as:

A powerful tool that helps you to quiet your emotions when they are out of control, to focus your thoughts when they are intrusive, and to reduce the amount of stress you experience.

To be more resilient, you need to be able to handle stress well. You can learn to prevent or minimize the amount of stress you experience by changing the way you think when confronted with stressors. But let's face it, you're not going to be able to avoid stress completely, so you also need a way to calm yourself down once stress takes over. That's where the calming techniques come into play.[202]

From a communication perspective, when people hear that I used to be a hostage negotiator[203] and am currently a crisis counselor,[204] they sometimes say they'd make a great negotiator or counselor in crisis situations because they are a "good talker."

Unfortunately, they are misinformed, as any great instructor or practitioner of those two professions knows that what makes those experts effective is something other than their ability to talk. It is listening, and more accurately, it is active listening. Silence is critical to listening, as it does two things: it helps you gather information and allows you to demonstrate empathy and build rapport.

The great, retired former FBI chief negotiator Gary Noesner explains the vital role listening plays:

We all need to be good listeners and learn to demonstrate our empathy and understanding of the problems, needs, and issues of others.

Only then can we hope to influence their behavior in a positive way.[205]

So, listening effectively—while it helps the other person feel understood— is also strategic when you are seeking to influence others. Your silence can be powerful and helpful for both you and the person you are engaging.

Dr. Helen Riess refers to active listening as "empathic listening" and describes it this way:

Empathic listening means paying attention to another person, identifying her emotions, and responding with compassion and without judgment.

The basic principle behind empathic listening is to first try to understand the other person's perspective and then try to have your own point of view understood.[206]

The order mentioned by Riess is critical. Seek to understand first before seeking to be understood. Listening to the person first allows their tense emotions to be reduced and lets them know they have been heard and understood. This allows them to be more open to listening to you next.

Try to remember, too, that practicing silent exercises like controlled breathing is not limited to only when tough, stressful moments arise. It is about the daily practice to wire the brain so it becomes a habit and part of your everyday living.

Jeremy Dean explains this importance in connection to yesterday's keyword, mindfulness, along with meditation:

Mindfulness is all about increasing your conscious awareness of what you are doing right now. It's often talked about in the context of meditation, but really, it is a way of life or an attitude.[207]

Dan Harris and his team remind us of how practices in silence like meditation (controlled breathing) is even for "dummies" (don't worry, I'm not calling you a dummy!):

Meditation is like life skills for dummies. I am a supreme dummy. The big picture overwhelms me. It makes me race around like a headless chicken spewing out explanations and trying to think my way to a neat "conclusion," at which point everything will be fine, forever. This isn't a bad working definition of insanity.

The genius of meditation is that it basically says: "*Hey, relax, bud, all you need to worry about is this moment. Can you find some focus? Some friendliness? A bit of perspective?*" Yes I can, meditation, thank you. And guess what? String together enough moments, you get life. Go figure.[208]

I'll end on a personal note. I've learned from experience that silence is incredibly effective at building my inner strength, resilience, and positive mental health. I've learned to let the other person get the last word. I've learned to not always jump in and give my opinion and my perspective or correct people even if I know they are wrong. I've learned that I don't have to say something even if I think I really am the smartest person in the room. I've learned that personal practices in silence bring me moments of genuine peace and calm.

It's day 20, **warr;ors**. This journey first started with me developing it and taking it myself. Today's keyword is something I continually struggle with and work on. It reminds me I haven't finished my journey, even after the initial twenty-one days, but it also reminds me that when I practice it each day, it helps me be a better person to me and to friends, family, and strangers.

Reflection

Take a few minutes at some point during your day to practice any type of silence that you have learned in the past twenty days. It can be a walk outside, sitting, or even turning off your music during your commute to work or school.

Also, engage someone in conversation. Try practicing silence and letting them talk. Genuinely listen and try to avoid interrupting them. Remember to embrace silence by giving them time (not awkwardly) to speak and collect their thoughts.

Finally, you are now entering the last days of **war;or21**. Enjoy it, relax, and make sure to take some time to enjoy yourself with family and friends, but also include moments of silence.

Evening Practice

In your notebook, write down answers to the following questions, remembering not to repeat your previous responses:

1. One thing that made you happy today
2. One nice thing someone did for you today
3. One nice thing you did for someone today
4. One thing that put you in awe today

Day 21: Journey (Conclusion)

Life is about accepting the challenges along
the way, choosing to keep moving forward, and savoring the journey.
—Roy T. Bennett

Morning Breathing Practice

Make it count, **warr;or.**

- As early as possible after you wake up, dedicate five minutes to breathing to help you get focused for the day and realize that you are setting your perspective.
- Start off with one minute of either the four-by-four or four-by-six breathing; it's your choice.
- Next, do the 4-7-8 breathing exercise.[209]
- Finish with two more minutes of either the four-by-four or four-by-six breathing.

  o Tell yourself before starting that you are deciding to do this because you want to and it is important to you.
  o Then, while doing it, enjoy it during the final two minutes.
  o Finally, at the end, remind yourself that you just accomplished something, especially here on day 21, and it was all because you made the time to do it. That should feel good!

REMEMBER, THIS IS NOT A soft program. It was designed for real people doing real work. There's no mushy conclusion here. Get that straight. If you're reading this, you earned it. Let there be no mistake about it. Tell yourself (really), "You earned this."

There is always realistic optimism. The purpose of this program was not to sell some unrealistic new reality but instead to give you a pathway to create new habits and a perspective to better handle life, stressors, and tense situations. It has been an opportunity to be better at what you are already good at. This is the meaning of "this is the way."

You're a **warr;or.**

You've built a stronger sense of resilience and a greater, real sense of positive mental health. You've intensified your inner strength and deepened your focus. You've smiled.

What we preach to others regarding positive mental health and building resilience starts with ourselves. What is good for others must also be good for us.

It can't be just words; it has to be real, and it has to be more than practice now at day 21.

It's a change—a change for the better.

Your journey over the past twenty-one days has demonstrated you took it beyond words; you made it your actions as well. You know creating positive habits is not easy. Yet you also know it is possible because you actually did it.

Take a moment and reflect on what you have accomplished. Seriously, reflect and share a smile with yourself. You proved to yourself you could do it. I hope your feelings and emotions include those of feeling empowered, positive, calmer, happier, and even perhaps a bit of relief.

Why relief? The journey is over.

The reality is you have created new habits, but maintaining it at this pace over many more days was never the focus or the plan of **warr;or21**. You started with a certain mind-set and perspective on day 0, and it is safe to say that your mind-set and perspective have changed over the course of twenty-one days.

Much like any journey, it has a beginning, the path itself, and then a conclusion. If you picture it as starting on one side of a shore, **warr;or21** is the raft that has helped you get to the other side. Now that you are here, it is time to discard the raft. You've made it here, and now it's time for a new journey.

Note, I'm not saying to abandon your **warr;or21** practices and forget these twenty-one days. It's actually the opposite. Take everything you have learned with you as you as continue on to new journeys, letting it guide you.

Yes, these twenty-one days have ended, but let their impact continue to ripple long past today and the days to come. As you go on new journeys, you can come back to these practices because you know there truly is no finish line. There is progress, yet also allow yourself to have setbacks. Setbacks are part of living, and I'm certain you had some during your **warr;or21** journey; that's normal.

That is human, after all.

Remember, too, we are not on these journeys alone. We have one other, and we must look out for one another. Let your practices from **warr;or21**

Jeff Thompson, Ph.D.

be a demonstration that positive change is possible. If you can do it, you will show others that they can do it as well.

Before you move forward and let go of your raft, take some time to reflect. Look through your notebook. It is a demonstration of your commitment to enhancing your resilience, your positive mental health, and your awareness of something to be grateful for every day.

The struggles you might have faced on certain days with varying practices were real too and not easy, much like the struggles you have faced throughout your life.

Yet you're still here.

You're still reading these words.

That's resilience. That's you taking care of your mental health. And that's impressive. Well done. Take a moment to reflect on your goals that you wrote in the beginning. Also, look back through your notebook at your gratitude practices. Yes, there are struggles in life, yet there are also good things happening every day. Never forget that. Seriously—never, ever forget that.

We know that repeated practices become habits. Even if we don't recall the specific research, we all know there is plenty of neuroscience research that shows that. As you start new journeys, let these practices help you stay on your path. Don't forget, let it start with your breathing practices. That is your foundation, and that is what will help you with every next step.

You now see things a bit clearer, you have better management over your emotions, and you respond (not react) to situations—especially ones that you did not expect.

Finally, remember that **warr;or21** doesn't stop with this internal focus and purpose; instead, your actions demonstrate that taking care of yourself is not in conflict with helping others.

Taking care of yourself first lets you then help others. That, too, is your purpose. The **warr;or** path starts internally, and as you move forward, it is to help more than just yourself. You got this! Onward you go.

Reflection

Think about the journey you have been on. Go back and look at the keywords that have impacted you the most. You are nearly at the end. Have one more conversation with someone now that you are on the last day of the **warr;or21** journey. Share with them what it meant to you. Take in their responses, knowing they haven't been on it. Don't judge while reflecting on how you explain it. There's no right or wrong way to explain it; it's your experience.

In one sentence, share on social media (only if you want) what this program has meant to you using the #warrior21days tag.

Evening Practice

In your notebook, write down answers to the following questions, remembering not to repeat your previous responses:

1. One thing that made you happy today
2. One nice thing someone did for you today
3. One nice thing you did for someone today
4. One thing that put you in awe today
5. One word to describe doing this **warr;or21** journey

I thought I'd share my gratitude practice with you today. It is from when I first finished writing this program and completed this last day:

1. I am happy you made it to today.
2. You made it to this point. Thank you for trusting me and taking this journey.
3. I worked on editing this up until the night before the first ever cohort so they could have a day 21 that was meaningful (for you now as well).
4. I looked at a flower on my porch, one that I never paid any attention to before. The sun setting behind it made the flower, leaves, and stem glow in a brilliant way. I found myself looking at it in awe for a few moments. The flower had always been there, but today I noticed it, and I observed it in a way that caught my attention.
5. I feel *accomplished*.

Congratulations! You are a **warr;or**. You always have been. Let these new tools, keywords, reflections, and practices help you go forward.

Onward!

Breathing Practices

Four-by-Four Breathing and Four-by-Six Breathing

Exhale the air in your lungs.

Breathe in through your nose for four seconds and then exhale through your nose for four seconds (eventually try to do the exhale for six seconds). When you breathe in and out, do it so that your stomach area expands and contracts (not your chest area).

You can see the guided breathing exercise for this at www.warrior21.com.

Mindful Breathing

This type of breathing exercise entails breathing naturally and concentrating solely on you breathing. As an added option, you can place one of your hands on your stomach area while doing this.

Guided/Keyword Breathing

Breathe in for four seconds and then out for four seconds, like above, but connect the in and out breaths with a positive, strong word or statement during the exhale. For example, when you breathe in, you can say in your head, "I am calm," and as you exhale, "I am at ease."

Other keywords can be focused/alert, relaxed/still, strong/still, happy/smile, and alive/energized. Come up with your own too.

Note: Stick with the same two words for an entire minute. Add more minutes and switch the words if you'd like.

Imagery Breathing Exercise

Breathe naturally and think of a favorite place you enjoy going to. Shortly, you will close your eyes, picturing it. As you do, experience it with your senses.

- o   What are four things you see?
- o   What are three different things you can touch? What does each feel like?
- o   What are two different things you can hear?
- o   What is one thing you can smell?
- o   Finally, describe how you feel while experiencing this.

4-7-8 Breathing

During the entire breathing exercise below, rest the front/tip of your tongue on the roof of your mouth just behind your front, top teeth.

Start by taking a deep breath (approximately four seconds) through the nose and exhale through your diaphragm (stomach area) for four to six seconds. Now ...

1)   Breathe through your nose for four seconds, filing your stomach area.

2)   Hold your breath for seven seconds.

3) Exhale your breath for eight seconds. While you exhale, purse your lips similarly to how they would be if you had a straw in your mouth but just a little looser than that. As you exhale for the eight seconds, make a slight whoosh sound as you let all of the air out over the eight seconds.

4) Try doing this for four rounds.

This technique, like other controlled breathing exercises, can help relax you, increase your focus, replenish the oxygen in your body, and ease stress and anxiety. Some use this exercise to help them fall asleep, while others use it to help them be alert and refreshed. Like any new exercise, it takes practice, and it also takes time to start feeling its impact.

These breathing exercises are generally safe and can improve health. However, they may trigger symptoms for those with certain medical or mental health conditions or for anyone with a history of abuse or trauma.

Talk with your doctor first if you have any health concerns and continue to follow up with your doctor for the treatment of any medical condition.

Breathe

DAY 2
Cognitive Triangle

DAY 3

Calm

DAY 4

Grit

Gratitude

Pause (;)

DAY 7
Practice

DAY 8

Resilience

DAY 9

Wisdom

DAY 10
Emotions

DAY 11
Reflection

DAY 12

Stress

DAY 13
Empathy

DAY 14

Sympathy

DAY 15

Awe

DAY 16
Perspective

DAY 17

Smile

DAY 18

Adapt

DAY 19

Mindfulness

DAY 20
Silence

DAY 21
Journey and Conclusion

Endnotes

1   J. Thompson and J. M. Drew, "Warr;or21: A 21-Day Program to Enhance First Responder Resilience and Mental Health," *Frontiers in Psychology* 11 (2020): 2078, doi:10.3389/fpsyg.2020.02078.

2   J. Thompson and J. M. Drew, "Warr;or21: A 21-Day Program to Enhance First Responder Resilience."

3   J. Thompson, "Enhancing Resilience During the COVID-19 Pandemic: A Thematic Analysis and Evaluation of the Warr;or21 Program," *Journal of Community Safety and Well-Being* 5, no. 2 (2020): 51–56, https://doi.org/10.35502/jcswb.134.

4   J. Thompson, "Enhancing Resilience During the COVID-19 Pandemic."

5   C. André, "Proper Breathing Brings Better Health." *Scientific American* (2019), https://www.scientificamerican.com/article/proper-breathing-brings-better-health.

6   André, "Proper Breathing Brings."

7   L. Weiss, *How We Work: Live Your Purpose, Reclaim Your Sanity, and Embrace the Daily Grind* (New York, NY: Harper Wave, 2018), 162–163.

8   Weiss, *How We Work*, 163.

9   R. Hanson, *Hardwiring Happiness: The New Brain Science of Contentment, Calm, and Confidence* (New York, NY: Harmony Books, 2016), 182.

10   L. M. Abdelsayed, "CBT—The Cognitive Triangle," Smart Talk, 2018, https://smarttalktherapy.com/cbt-cognitive-triangle, opening paragraph.

11   S. J. Gillihan, *Retrain Your Brain: Cognitive Behavioral Therapy in 7 Weeks: A Workbook for Managing Depression and Anxiety* (New York, NY: Althea, 2016).

12   A. Korb, *The Upward Spiral: Using Neuroscience to Reverse the Course of Depression, One Small Change at a Time* (Oakland, CA: New Harbinger, 2015).

13   Hanson, *Hardwiring Happiness*, 13.

14   K. Reivich and A. Shatte, *The Resilience Factor: 7 Keys to Finding Your Inner Strength and Overcoming Life's Hurdles* (New York, NY: Harmony Books, 2003).

[15] J. M. Grohol, "10 Proven Methods for Fixing Cognitive Distortions," PsychCentral, 2018, https://psychcentral.com/lib/fixing-cognitive-distortions.

[16] Weiss, *How We Work*, 162.

[17] M. Fitzgerald, "Cognitive Triangle Worksheet," Medical University of South Carolina, https://depts.washington.edu/hcsats/PDF/TF-%20 CBT/pages/4%20Coping%20Skills/Thoughts/Cognitive%20 Triangle_Worksheet_Coping_and_Processing.pdf.

[18] Beck Institute, "Cognitive Model: Theory of Psychopathology," https://beck-institute.org/cognitive-model.

[19] C. Chu, "Bulletproof Mind: 6 Secrets of Mental Toughness from the Navy SEALs," 2016, Observer, https://observer.com/2016/11/bulletproof-mind-6-secrets-of-mental-toughness-from-the-navy-seals/.

[20] R. Hilmantel, "4 Signs You Have Grit," Time.com, May 12, 2016, https://time.com/4327035/4-signs-you-have-grit/, first paragraph.

[21] A. Duckworth, *Grit: The Power of Passion and Perseverance* (New York, NY: Scribner, 2016).

[22] Several are available here: https://www.bakadesuyo.com.

[23] E. Barker, "Inner Strength: This Is the Research-Backed Way to Increase Grit," 2016, https://www.bakadesuyo.com/2016/05/inner-strength, under "3) Find Purpose."

[24] Barker, "Inner Strength," same as above.

[25] Barker, "Inner Strength," under "Sum Up."

[26] A. Weil, "4-7-8 Breath Relaxation Exercise," 2010, Arizona Center for Integrative Medicine, https://www.cordem.org/globalassets/files/academic-assembly/2017-aa/handouts/day-three/biofeedback-exercises-for-stress-2---fernances-j.pdf.

[27] Korb, *The Upward Spiral*, 152.

[28] S. Allen, "The Science of Gratitude," 2018, a white paper prepared for the John Templeton Foundation by the Greater Good Science Center at UC Berkeley, https://ggsc.berkeley.edu/images/uploads/GGSC-JTF_White_Paper-Gratitude-FINAL.pdf.

[29] Korb, *The Upward Spiral*.

[30] D. Robson, "How a Daily 10-Minute Exercise Could Boost Your Happiness," 2018, BBC, https://www.bbc.com/future/article/20181016-how-to-boost-your-mood-with-one-10-minute-exercise.

[31] Robson, "How a Daily 10-Minute," fifth paragraph.

32 Y. Cohen, "5 Reasons Keeping a Gratitude Journal Will Change Your Life," 2017, https://www.goodnet.org/articles/5-reasons-keeping-gratitude-journal-will-change-your-life, under points 2, 3, and 4.

33 R. A. Emmons and M. E. McCullough, "Counting Blessings versus Burdens: An Experimental Investigation of Gratitude and Subjective Well-Being in Daily Life," *Journal of Personality and Social Psychology* 84, no. 2 (2003): 377–389, https://doi.org/10.1037/0022-3514.84.2.377.

34 A. Amin, "The 31 Benefits of Gratitude You Didn't Know About: How Gratitude Can Change Your Life," 2014, Happier Human, http://happierhuman.com/benefits-of-gratitude/.

35 B. J. Dik, R. D. Duffy, B. A. Allan, M. B. O'Donnell, Y. Shim, and M. F. Steger, "Purpose and Meaning in Career Development Applications," *Counseling Psychologist* 43 (2015): 558–585, doi:10.1177/0011000014546872.

36 J. Dean, *Making Habits, Breaking Habits: Why We Do Things, Why We Don't, and How to Make Any Change Stick* (Philadelphia, PA: De Capo Press, 2013).

37 J. Dean, "10 Easy Activities Science Has Proven Will Make You Happier Today," PsyBlog, https://www.spring.org.uk/2013/07/10-easy-activities-science-has-proven-will-make-you-happier-today.php, under point 8.

38 Weil, "4-7-8 Breath Relaxation Exercise."

39 https://projectsemicolon.com.

40 R. Gilkey and C. Kilts, "Cognitive Fitness," *Harvard Business Review* (2007), https://hbr.org/2007/11/cognitive-fitness, third paragraph under "Step 1."

41 Gillihan, *Retrain Your Brain*, 71.

42 Gillihan, *Retrain Your Brain*, 71.

43 R. Hanson, *Resilient: 12 Tools for Transforming Everyday Experiences into Lasting Happiness* (New York, NY: Harmony Books, 2018), 35, 39.

44 L. Willard, "Semicolon Tattoo: Here's What It Means and Why It Matters," Upworthy, 2015, https://www.upworthy.com/have-you-seen-anyone-with-a-semicolon-tattoo-heres-what-its-about.

45 Weil, "4-7-8 Breath Relaxation Exercise."

46 MulliganBrothers, *Arnold Schwarzenegger 2018—The Speech That Broke the Internet—Most Inspiring Ever*, 2019, https://www.youtube.com/watch?v=u_ktRTWMX3M.

47 Gilkey & Kilts, "Cognitive Fitness," seventh paragraph.

48 R. Hilmantel, "4 Signs You Have Grit," 2016, https://time.com/4327035/4-signs-you-have-grit/, under "2. You view frustrations as a necessary part of the process."

49   Hilmantel, "4 Signs," second paragraph.

50   Weil, "4-7-8 Breath Relaxation Exercise."

51   H. Deutschendorf, "7 Habits of Highly Resilient People," Fast Company, 2015, https://www.fastcompany.com/3041723/7-habits-of-highly-resilient-people, under "6. Are selective in whom they look for guidance and inspiration."

52   K. Reivich, "The Main Ingredients of Resilience," http://www.centreforconfidence.co.uk/pp/overview.php?p=c2lkPTUmdGlkPTAmaWQ9MTEz, under "7. Reaching out."

53   J. D. Margolis and P. Stoltz, "How to Bounce Back from Adversity," *Harvard Business Review* (2010), https://hbr.org/2010/01/how-to-bounce-back-from-adversity, under the title "The Capacity for Resilience."

54   L. Graham, *Bouncing Back: Rewiring Your Brain for Maximum Resilience and Well-Being* (Novato, CA: New World Library, 2013), 12.

55   Margolis and Stoltz, "How to Bounce Back," under "Control."

56   Hanson, *Resilient*, 47.

57   Hanson, *Resilient*, 79.

58   Hanson, *Resilient*, 79.

59   Weil, "4-7-8 Breath Relaxation Exercise."

60   Weiss, *How We Work*, 186.

61   Weiss, *How We Work*, 189–190.

62   Gillihan, *Retrain your brain*, 175.

63   E. Barker, "The 4 Rituals That Will Make You an Expert at Anything," 2016, https://www.bakadesuyo.com/2016/03/expert/.

64   Barker, "The 4 Rituals," under "3) It's about doing, not knowing."

65   N. Cole, "5 Daily Habits That Will Cultivate a Positive Mindset," 2016, https://www.inc.com/nicolas-cole/5-ways-to-cultivate-a-positive-mindset.html, under "1. Make time for input."

66   Cole, "5 Daily Habits," under "2. Read, read, read."

67   Cole, "5 Daily Habits," under "3. Surround yourself with positive people."

68   Cole, "5 Daily Habits," under "4. Practice."

69   Cole, "5 Daily Habits," under "4. Practice."

70   Cole, "5 Daily Habits," under "5. Find a mentor."

71   Much of this is adapted from https://www.winona.edu/resilience.

72   Weil, "4-7-8 Breath Relaxation Exercise."

73   Hanson, *Hardwiring Happiness*, 81.

74   Hanson, *Hardwiring Happiness*, 81.

75 D. DeSteno, *Emotional Success: The Power of Gratitude, Compassion, and Pride* (New York, NY: Eamon Dolan/Houghton Mifflin Harcourt, 2018), 91.

76 Weiss, *How We Work*, 161.

77 Weiss, *How We Work*, 152, 154.

78 L. Weiss, "A Simple Way to Stay Grounded in Stressful Moments," *Harvard Business Review* (2016), https://hbr.org/2016/11/a-simple-way-to-stay-grounded-in-stressful-moments, section under "pay attention to emotions."

79 DeSteno, *Emotional Success*, 6–7.

80 DeSteno, *Emotional Success*, 7.

81 S. M. Southwick and D. S. Charney, *Resilience: The Science of Mastering Life's Greatest Challenges* (Cambridge, UK: Cambridge University, 2018), 43.

82 J. Thompson, "Active Listening Techniques of Hostage & Crisis Negotiators," *Psychology Today* (2013), https://www.psychologytoday.com/us/blog/beyond-words/201311/active-listening-techniques-hostage-crisis-negotiators.

83 J. Thompson, "Crisis Counselor Skills: Helping People in Crisis … In 160 Characters or Less, 2018, https://www.mediate.com/articles/thompson-crisis-counselor.cfm.

84 Korb, *The Upward Spiral*, 147.

85 Weil, "4-7-8 Breath Relaxation Exercise."

86 J. Dean, "A Sense of Purpose Helps You Live Longer," PsyBlog, 2014, https://www.spring.org.uk/2014/05/a-sense-of-purpose-helps-you-live-longer.php, in the opening two paragraphs.

87 Korb, *The Upward Spiral*, 129.

88 Korb, *The Upward Spiral*, 129.

89 Neff, *Self-Compassion* (New York, NY: William Morrow, 2015), 152–153.

90 S. D. Young, *Stick with It: A Scientifically Proven Process for Changing Your Life—For Good* (New York, NY: Harper, 2017).

91 Young, *Stick with It*, 9–10.

92 Korb, *The Upward Spiral*, 104.

93 Korb, *The Upward Spiral*, 104.

94 Weil, "4-7-8 Breath Relaxation Exercise."

95 Mao Clinic staff, "Stress Symptoms: Effects on Your Body and Behavior," 2019, https://www.mayoclinic.org/healthy-lifestyle/stress-management/in-depth/stress-symptoms/art-20050987.

96 A. Crum and T. Crum, "Stress Can Be a Good Thing if You Know How to Use It," *Harvard Business Review* (2015), https://hbr.org/2015/09/stress-can-be-a-good-thing-if-you-know-how-to-use-it, third paragraph.

97 Crum & Crum, "Stress Can Be," under "Step One."

98 Crum & Crum, "Stress Can Be," under "Step Two."

99 Crum & Crum, "Stress Can Be," under "Step Three."

100 A. Clarke, "How to Harness Your Anxiety," *New York Times*, 2018, https://www.nytimes.com/2018/10/16/well/mind/how-to-harness-your-anxiety.html, third paragraph.

101 Clarke, "How to Harness," seventh paragraph.

102 Clarke, "How to Harness," seventh paragraph.

103 Clarke, "How to Harness," under "2. Label the feeling to steer your experience."

104 Korb, *The Upward Spiral*, 147.

105 Korb, *The Upward Spiral*, 147.

106 Crum & Crum, "Stress Can Be," third paragraph under "Step Three: Use It."

107 Crum & Crum, "Stress Can Be," last paragraph.

108 Weil, "4-7-8 Breath Relaxation Exercise."

109 H. Riess and L. Neporent, *The Empathy Effect: Seven Neuroscience-Based Keys for Transforming the Way We Live, Love, Work, and Connect across Differences* (Boulder, CO: Sounds True, 2018).

110 J. Bariso, "There Are Actually 3 Types of Empathy. Here's How They Differ—And How You Can Develop Them All," 2018, https://www.inc.com/justin-bariso/there-are-actually-3-types-of-empathy-heres-how-they-differ-and-how-you-can-develop-them-all.html, under "What empathy is (and what it is not)."

111 J. Suttie, "Why the World Needs an Empathy Revolution," 2019, https://greatergood.berkeley.edu/article/item/why_the_world_needs_an_empathy_revolution, under "Empathy can be taught."

112 http://empathetics.com/the-empathy-effect/, second paragraph.

113 E. Seppälä, "8 Ways Your Body Speaks Way Louder Than Your Words," 2017, https://www.psychologytoday.com/us/blog/feeling-it/201704/8-ways-your-body-speaks-way-louder-your-words, points 6 and 7 under "The Key: Body Language."

114 Online sources include J. Thompson, "Law Enforcement Suicide: How Police and First-Responders Can Support One Another's Mental Health," American Foundation for Suicide Prevention, 2019, https://afsp.org/law-enforcement-suicide-how-police-and-first-responders-can-support-one-anothers-mental-health; Thompson, "Crisis Counselor Skills."

115 https://www.mentalhealthfirstaid.org.

116 https://www.crisistextline.org/volunteer.

117 Weil, "4-7-8 Breath Relaxation Exercise."

118 P. Cohen, "Humans Are Hardwired to Feel Others' Pain," 2004, https://www.newscientist.com/article/dn4700-humans-are-hardwired-to-feel-others-pain/.

119 A. Womble, *Everything Is Going to Be OK: A Real Talk Guide for Living Well with Mental Illness* (New York, NY: Magical Thinking Media, 2018), 150.

120 Neff, *Self-Compassion,* 152, 153.

121 Riess & Neporent, *The Empathy Effect,* 53.

122 A. Boyes, *The Healthy Mind Toolkit: Simple Strategies to Get Out of Your Own Way and Enjoy Your Life* (New York, NY: TarcherPerigeem, 2018), 67.

123 Boyes, *The Healthy Mind Toolkit,* 67.

124 "Compassion defined," https://greatergood.berkeley.edu/topic/compassion/definition, second and third paragraphs.

125 Weil, "4-7-8 Breath Relaxation Exercise."

126 S. DiGiulo, "Why Scientists Say Experiencing Awe Can Help You Live Your Best life," 2019, https://www.nbcnews.com/better/lifestyle/why-scientists-say-experiencing-awe-can-help-you-live-your-ncna961826, fourth paragraph.

127 DiGiulo, "Why Scientists Say," fifth paragraph.

128 M. Shiota, "Research That Takes Your Breath Away: The Impact of Awe," Arizona State University, 2019, https://asunow.asu.edu/20190103-research-takes-your-breath-away-impact-awe, first paragraph.

129 DiGiulo, "Why Scientists Say," fourth paragraph under "How experiencing awe bears on wellbeing."

130 DiGiulo, "Why Scientists Say."

131 E. Stone, "The Emerging Science of Awe and Its Benefits," *Psychology Today* (2017), https://www.psychologytoday.com/gb/blog/understanding-awe/201704/the-emerging-science-awe-and-its-benefits.

132 Shiota, "Research That Takes," fourth paragraph under "The Gucci handbag of emotions: Awe is not an emotional luxury."

133 C. Bergland, "The Power of Awe: A Sense of Wonder Promotes Loving-Kindness," *Psychology Today* (2015), https://www.psychologytoday.com/intl/blog/the-athletes-way/201505/the-power-awe-sense-wonder-promotes-loving-kindness, first paragraph under "What Experiences Elicit a Sense of Awe for You?"

134 Bergland, "The power of Awe," seventh paragraph.

135 D. Kelter, "Why Do We Feel Awe?" 2016, https://greatergood.berkeley.edu/article/item/why_do_we_feel_awe, last paragraph.

136 https://afsp.org.

[137] Thompson, "Law Enforcement Suicide."

[138] J. Thompson, "Crisis Negotiation: How to Talk to Someone You're Worried About," American Foundation for Suicide Prevention, https://afsp.org/crisis-negotiation-talk-someone-youre-worried.

[139] American Foundation for Suicide Prevention, "How to Start (and Continue!) a Conversation about Mental Health: A #RealConvo Guide from AFSP," https://afsp.org/how-to-start-and-continue-a-conversation-about-mental-health-a-real-convo-guide-from-afsp.

[140] https://www.nami.org/Learn-More/Mental-Health-Conditions.

[141] https://suicidology.org.

[142] Weil, "4-7-8 Breath Relaxation Exercise."

[143] Korb, *The Upward Spiral*, 132.

[144] K. Harding, *The Rabbit Effect: Live Longer, Happier, and Healthier with the Groundbreaking Science of Kindness* (New York, NY: Atria, 2019), 166.

[145] Harding, *The Rabbit Effect*, 167.

[146] Hanson, *Hardwiring Happiness*, 101.

[147] Reivich & Shatte, *The Resilience Factor*, 91.

[148] For more, see http://www.dartmouth.edu/eap/abcstress2.pdf.

[149] Reivich & Shatte, *The Resilience Factor*, 91.

[150] S. M. Southwick and D. S. Charney, *Resilience: The Science of Mastering Life's Greatest Challenges* (Cambridge, UK: Cambridge University, 2018), 234.

[151] Southwick & Charney, *Resilience*, 234.

[152] Reivich & Shatte, *The Resilience Factor*, 56.

[153] Southwick & Charney, *Resilience*, 40.

[154] Southwick & Charney, *Resilience*, 51.

[155] Hanson, *Hardwiring Happiness*, 180.

[156] Weil, "4-7-8 Breath Relaxation Exercise."

[157] E. Bernstein, "'Self talk': When Talking to Yourself, the Way You Do It Makes a Difference," *Wall Street Journal*, 2014, https://www.wsj.com/articles/self-talk-when-talking-to-yourself-the-way-you-do-it-makes-a-difference-1399330343.

[158] S. Y. Morris, "What Are the Benefits of Self-Talk?" 2016, https://www.healthline.com/health/mental-health/self-talk, third paragraph under "Language matters."

[159] M. Stibich, "Top 10 Reasons You Should Smile Every Day," 2020, https://www.verywellmind.com/top-reasons-to-smile-every-day-2223755.

160 N. Spector, "Smiling Can Trick Your Brain into Happiness—And Boost Your Health," 2017, https://www.nbcnews.com/better/health/smiling-can-trick-you r-brain-happiness-boost-your-health-ncna822591, first paragraph.

161 M. Brilaki, "How to Think Happy Thoughts and Train Your Brain to Be Happy," Lifehack, 2020, https://www.lifehack.org/articles/communication/how-train-your-brain-happy.html, under "4. Add a "But" to Turn Your Unhappiness Into Happiness."

162 Dean, "10 Easy Activities Science Has Proven Will Make You Happier Today" https://www.spring.org.uk/2013/07/10-easy-activities-science-has-pro ven-will-make-you-happier-today.php, under "5. Listen to music."

163 Harding, "How a Study on Rabbits Revealed the Secret to Living a Longer Life," *NY Post*, 2019, https://nypost.com/2019/08/24/how-a-study-on-rabbit s-revealed-the-secret-to-living-a-longer-life/, nineteenth paragraph.

164 Hanson, *Hardwiring Happiness*,190.

165 Weil, "4-7-8 Breath Relaxation Exercise."

166 Southwick & Charney, *Resilience*.

167 Weiss, *How We Work*.

168 M. L. Marks, P. Mirvis, et al., "Rebounding from Career Setbacks," *Harvard Business Review* (2014), https://hbr.org/2014/10/rebounding-from-career -setbacks.

169 Weiss, *How We Work*, 14.

170 Weiss, *How We Work,* 179

171 M. E. P. Seligman, T. Schwartz et al., *HBR's 10 Must Reads on Mental Toughness* (Boston, MA: Harvard Business Review, 2018), 27.

172 Marks, Mirvis, et al., "Rebounding from Career Setbacks," under "Figure out why you lost."

173 Gilkey & Kilts, "Cognitive Fitness," seventh paragraph.

174 Korb, *The Upward Spiral.*

175 S. Sideroff, "Resilience and Restoring Your Ability to Adapt," *Psychology Today* (2015), https://www.psychologytoday.com/us/blog/ path-optimal-living/201510/resilience-and-restoring-your-ability-adapt, second to last paragraph.

176 Korb, *The Upward Spiral.*

177 Reivich & Shatte, *The Resilience Factor.*

178 Southwick & Charney, *Resilience.*

179 Korb, *The Upward Spiral*, 104.

180 Weil, "4-7-8 Breath Relaxation Exercise."

181 S. M. Conn, *Increasing Resilience in Police and Emergency Personnel* (London, UK: Routledge, 2018), 163.

182 M. Richtel, "The Latest in Military Strategy: Mindfulness," *New York Times*, 2019, https://www.nytimes.com/2019/04/05/health/military-mindfulness-training.html, tenth paragraph.

183 Conn, *Increasing Resilience*, 163.

184 Weiss, *How We Work*.

185 Weiss, *How We Work*.

186 Weiss, *How We Work*.

187 Southwick & Charney, *Resilience*, 208.

188 Southwick & Charney, *Resilience*, 208.

189 S. J. Gillihan, *Cognitive Behavioral Therapy Made Simple: 10 Strategies for Managing Anxiety, Depression, Anger, Panic, and Worry* (New York, NY: Althea, 2018), 92.

190 J. Suttie, "Five Ways Mindfulness Meditation Is Good for Your Health," *Greater Good* (2018), https://greatergood.berkeley.edu/article/item/five_ways_mindfulness_meditation_is_good_for_your_health, second paragraph under "Mindfulness may help reduce psychological pain."

191 Weil, "4-7-8 Breath Relaxation Exercise."

192 L. Morrison, "The Subtle Power of Uncomfortable Silences," BBC, 2017, https://www.bbc.com/worklife/article/20170718-the-subtle-power-of-uncomfortable-silences.

193 Australian Academy of Science, "It's Just Noise … Right?" 2017, https://www.science.org.au/curious/earth-environment/health-effects-environmental-noise-pollution.

194 World Health Organization, "Burden of Disease from Environmental Noise: Quantification of Healthy Life Years Lost In Europe," 2011, https://www.who.int/quantifying_ehimpacts/publications/e94888.pdf.

195 Weiss, *How We Work*.

196 S. Kane, "The Hidden Benefits of Silence," PsycheCentral, 2018, https://psychcentral.com/blog/the-hidden-benefits-of-silence.

197 L. Bernardi, C. Porta, et al., "Cardiovascular, Cerebrovascular, and Respiratory Changes Induced by Different Types of Music in Musicians and Non-Musicians: The Importance of Silence," *Heart* 92, no. 4 (2006): 445–452.

198 A. Kramer and M. Gatz, "Growing a Bigger Brain Is a Walk in the Park," 2011, https://www.npr.org/2011/02/04/133498136/growing-a-bigger-brain-is-a-walk-in-the-park.

[199] J. Schooler, "Jonathan Schooler," 2018, https://www.psych.ucsb.edu/people/faculty/jonathan-schooler.

[200] T. Nguyen, "10 Important Reasons to Start Making Time for Silence, Rest and Solitude," *Huffington Post*, 2014, https://www.huffpost.com/entry/10-important-reasons-to-s_b_6035662.

[201] R. Berris, "Science Says Silence Is Much More Important to Our Brains Than We Think," Lifehack, 2019, https://www.lifehack.org/377243/science-says-silence-much-more-important-our-brains-than-thought.

[202] Reivich & Shatte, *The Resilience Factor*, 192.

[203] Pon staff, "Police Negotiation Techniques from the NYPD Crisis Negotiations Team. Program on Negotiation," 2019, https://www.pon.harvard.edu/daily/crisis-negotiations/crisis-negotiations-and-negotiation-skills-insights-from-the-new-york-city-police-department-hostage-negotiations-team.

[204] Thompson, "Crisis Counselor Skills."

[205] G. Noesner, *Stalling for Time: My Life as an FBI Hostage Negotiator* (New York, NY: Random House, 2010), 216.

[206] Riess & Neporent, *The Empathy Effect*, 55.

[207] J. Dean, *Making Habits, Breaking Habits: Why We Do Things, Why We Don't, and How to Make Any Change Stick* (Philadelphia, PA: De Capo Press, 2013).

[208] D. Harris, J. Warren, et al., *Meditation for Fidgety Skeptics: A 10% Happier How-To Book* (New York, NY: Spiegel & Grau, 2018), 221.

[209] Weil, "4-7-8 Breath Relaxation Exercise."

Index

#Warrior21Days
Twitter: @warrior21days
Instagram: @warrior21days
www.warrior21.com

Made in United States
North Haven, CT
11 September 2023

41437045R00134